CONDUCT OF THE MIND SERIES
EDITED BY
JOSEPH JASTROW

PSYCHOLOGY
IN DAILY LIFE

THE CONDUCT OF MIND SERIES

Edited By Joseph Jastrow, Ph.D.

VOCATIONAL PSYCHOLOGY
By H. L. HOLLINGWORTH, PH.D.

CHARACTER AND TEMPERAMENT
By JOSEPH JASTROW, PH.D.

PSYCHOLOGY IN DAILY LIFE
By C. E. SEASHORE, PH.D.

MENTAL ADJUSTMENTS
By FREDERIC LYMAN WELLS, PH.D.

D. APPLETON & COMPANY
Publishers   **NEW YORK**

212

PSYCHOLOGY IN DAILY LIFE

BY

CARL EMIL SEASHORE

PROFESSOR OF PSYCHOLOGY AND DEAN OF THE GRADUATE COLLEGE
IN THE STATE UNIVERSITY OF IOWA

NEW YORK AND LONDON
D. APPLETON AND COMPANY
1918

INTRODUCTION TO THE CONDUCT OF MIND SERIES

It is the purpose of the series to provide readily intelligible surveys of selected aspects of the study of mind and of its applications. In this self-conscious age, inquiring minutely into the nature of the forces that direct the endeavors of men, psychology has come to its own. Recent advances have made possible definite and enlightening accounts of the mental processes; the psychological laboratory has refined, extended, and controlled the data; the evolutionary conception has coördinated conclusions derived from widely different sources. Particularly has the psychology of the social relations been given a central position in the practical world, where endowment, motive, and circumstance meet. The emotional as well as the intellectual, the æsthetic as well as the moral, the occupational as well as the relational impulses and expressions of men have been duly recognized as part of the psychological endowment—as integral aspects of human nature.

INTRODUCTION TO SERIES

The desire to apply this knowledge reflects the stress of the practical temper; the need of adaptation of the mental equipment to the complex conditions of modern life is insistent. Mental economy enforces the importance of shaping career to capacity; the conservation of mental resources enters vitally into the problems of national welfare. The varied liability of the mind to defect and decay, to distortion and vagary, to degeneration and reversion, sets in relief the critical importance of sanity, which is a eugenic endowment exercised in a wholesome environment. From these several sources there has resulted a sense of psychological value by which to gauge the worth of the educational and cultural provisions which society organizes for the maintenance of its cherished ends. Furthermore, the ready intercourse of mankind has conferred a cosmopolitan and an humanitarian outlook, mingling and comparing, while yet contrasting, national and local standards and ideals. The products of intellectual, as of other achievements, are seen to belong not to one race or to one era or to one order of culture. The beginnings of mind in the animal world, the growth of mind in childhood and in the race, contribute notably to broaden the conception of its mature capacity and its potential future.

INTRODUCTION TO SERIES

To set forth and interpret the significant conclusions within this engaging realm forms the dominant motive of the present undertaking. The project, if too ambitiously conceived, invites failure. The practicable procedure favors the selection of a modest aspect or phase of the psychological domain, and its presentation as a concrete distribution upon which the larger illumination of a comprehensive survey has been brought to bear. The importance of principle is to be emphasized throughout. In simpler situations a shrewd empirical tact suffices; in complex ones sound practice is more and more dependent upon sound theory. Knowledge of principles is needed to offset the limitations of experience and the narrowness of interests; the corrective of application is needed to make principles real and vital. The search for panaceas as for rules of thumb is futile; yet the desire for a royal road to learning has a strange attraction for the direct democratic temper. Psychology, like all science, exacts a patient analysis, which discountenances a too ready leap at conclusions and hasty application. Yet science does well to utilize the actual interests of men to build upon them the knowledge that makes for power. To supply the foundation in principle for the guidance of practice is to be the consistent motive in the several volumes of the

INTRODUCTION TO SERIES

series. To make that guidance effective requires a judicious appeal to popular interest, and an adaptation of the material to the needs of the every-day reader with serious purpose.

To give the largest freedom in adapting the presentation to the varied requirements of the several topics and the individual bent of the contributors, it is proposed to permit the volumes to assume such length, form, and construction as circumstances determine. The singleness of purpose and unity of design will appear in the support of each contribution to the general plan, and in their common appeal to the popular interests in the affairs of the world of mind, in the regulation of mental conduct.

JOSEPH JASTROW

INTRODUCTION

The present volume follows the general plan of the "Conduct of Mind" series, which is to interpret selected areas of the mental domain, and to bring the relevant principles to bear upon popular interests and practical concerns. The illumination of practice by principle in matters psychological, is the keynote of the undertaking. By the nature of the subject the unity of the present volume is selective rather than consecutive; the common bearing of the exposition is directed to the expressions of mental procedure in ordinary activities. An appeal is made to varied types of interests, suggestive, also, of wider application. The closer study of a typical mental product serves to bring forward relations not apparent in a superficial survey. This is desirable in that the psychological excursion—here personally conducted by an able exponent—lies for the most part in a region of fair familiarity. To see familiar things in a new relation, to penetrate a little deeper into their meaning, is often quite as profitable as to tour through new territory with opportunity only for casual observation. The volume combines both procedures.

The preëminence of the subject of "play" for illustrating psychological principles, as exercised in daily life, is apparent. Play goes back to the beginnings of intellectual spontaneity, and taps a source that vitalizes the mental life at all stages. It represents one of the most generic of mental attitudes. Its purest expression is characteristic of the early ages of life, in which impulse is less hampered by imposed purpose, and natural growth sets its own course. Obedient to the general principle that what lies deep persists, the impulse continues to infuse occupation with a peculiar quality. The spirit of play makes the game of life; the skill in exercising it makes the artist. Pursuits, however varied, however subject to other motives and obligations, conform to the primary patterns of mental activity. In a wholesome sense the introduction of the element of venture, of satisfaction in exercise, supports interest and conserves vigor. Conversely, the adaptation of occupation to the psychological nature will wisely follow the clue thus indicated.

Play in occupation, as in relaxation, fulfills its function in so far as it engages the whole man. The adult is capable of becoming absorbed in work, as is the child in play. The capacities drawn upon have undergone systematic training, and are directed to acquired desires replacing natural ones and involving composite satisfactions. Since such is the condition of the mental life, as we live it, we acquire an interest in the constituent processes that sustain our activities. In this group memory represents the conservative factor; it is selected as a type of the mental mechanism. Certain aspects of its operations are set forth, showing how we hold what we have gained, invest it in new venture, and direct it to further service. The subject leads naturally to the larger mental economy of which it forms a part. Efficiency becomes the test. The problem of the conduct of mind is presented as the regulation of work and play. Mental health results from the establishment of a psychological régime suited to the endowment and to the demands made upon it by the concerns of daily life. The process of living, which is real and earnest, enforces attention to the close adjustment of process to result. Psychology contributes a perspective in which essentials stand apart from details, and principles from minute application. It shows in how far the process is the same, however diverse the expression, in how far the problems are the same, though stated in different terms.

INTRODUCTION

The dominance of law in the expressions of the mental equipment receives a striking confirmation in the apparent exception to its rule, which we call an illusion. True perception, which maintains the organism in its relation to the environment, and illusion, which plays it false, are of one nature. A reliable adjustment to the usual involves liability to error in the presence of the unusual. The senses remain law-abiding, even when the exception is treated as the rule, or conflict of conditions entails confusion. If extended to complex situations, in which judgment and inference outweigh perception, the application to daily life becomes more direct and suggestive.

Every science develops a technique in pursuit of special problems. The results of the laboratory often seem remote from the occupations of men. The concluding chapter brings the two in relation. It selects a given range of endowment—that of musical ability—central in one of the professions and conditioning one of the great pleasures of life —and describes how the psychologist proceeds to take the measure thereof. The investigation acquaints the reader with the painstaking steps by which conclusions are established, shows the dependence of proficiency, vocational or otherwise,

INTRODUCTION

upon endowment, and the importance of accuracy in determining the basis thereof.

In such eclectic manner, but with a singleness of purpose, the volume covers certain areas of contact between the results of psychology and the practical expression of mental processes in current situations and occupations. The *rapprochement* will serve to quicken the appreciation of the message which psychology brings to daily life, to deepen understanding, and thereby extend control. The simple statement of the text and the familiarity of the range of illustration will recommend the volume to the increasing numbers of readers and students whose natural bent and occupation gives them an interest in the conduct of mind.

JOSEPH JASTROW

The University of Wisconsin,
    Madison, Wis.

PREFACE

The chapters of this volume were originally prepared as semi-public addresses to illustrate some applications of psychology. Although the content has been freely adapted and supplemented for the present purpose, the style of direct address has been retained in order to conserve, in the printed page, the character of a personal message from one in the technical workshop. For the same reason the lessons for life—economic, hygienic, pedagogical, ethical, æsthetical, religious—which are drawn from the psychological interpretation of common events are thrown into the foreground and often put in the form of a charge. Instead of writing *about* the uses of psychology the author has aimed to present actual bits of psychology in intensive illustrations with immediate application to daily life.

Parts of chapters have appeared in the journals: the section on the rôle of play in religion, in the *American Journal of Theology;* four of the illustrations on mental efficiency, in the *Journal of Edu-*

PREFACE

cational Psychology; and the gist of the illustration on the measure of a singer, in *Science.* The author is indebted to the publishers of these journals for the right to use this material.

C. E. S.
Iowa City, Iowa.
September 20, 1913.

CONTENTS

2   xvii

CONTENTS

PSYCHOLOGY IN DAILY LIFE

CHAPTER I

PLAY

The introduction of the method of natural history in psychology has transformed the conception of play—its nature, its function, its evolution, its meaning. With the deeper significance discovered in play comes a broader interpretation of education, knowledge, morality, art, and religion.

Play is free self-expression for the pleasure of expression; or, as Ruskin puts it, "an exertion of body or mind, made to please ourselves, and with no determined end." The radiations of the psychology of play are too extensive to be here considered in all their aspects. The present chapter will be limited to a survey of the practical bearings of play, showing something of its scope, its meaning, and its place in a psychological accounting of our nature.

PSYCHOLOGY IN DAILY LIFE

Children seldom play with the intention of fitting themselves for life, nor are adults ordinarily conscious of serving this purpose in play. Children play, as do the rest of us, because it satisfies certain cravings and seems to be the eternally fit and natural thing to do. It is only in the larger, retrospective view that we realize how nature has wrought marvels of development through the operation of the play instincts.

PLAY IS PREPARATION FOR LIFE

The senses develop largely through the play which their exercise invites. By play the infant discovers his ears, investigates his nose, "pat-a-cakes" with his hands, and splashes, fumbles, rubs, scratches, gropes, and grasps to feel himself and the objects about him. These semi-random touch-plays refine the sense of touch, develop ability in locating tactual impressions, and give meaning to these experiences by establishing and enriching associations; concomitantly they furnish pastime and amusement and develop the exercise of curiosity.

All sorts of ringing, rapping, shouting, sizzling, rattling, cracking, and jingling sounds appeal to the ear of the infant. Through such exercise the auditory interest, comprehension, and appreciation are gradually refined into a liking for higher forms of rhythm, accent, modulation, tone-quality, pitch, melody, and harmony. The child is first attracted by the louder sounds; through the mastery of these he acquires the power of appreciating the refinements of perception. At first all sounds are alike to him; their distinctive qualities are learned through play.

The playful production of sounds runs parallel with the growing appreciation of sounds. The ability to make sounds is a continual source of pleasure and profit. There is a close connection and a gradual transition from the youngster's racket and howl to the set and studied piano exercise and the lesson in voice-culture. The mastery of the voice is acquired far more by play than by conscious and purposeful effort.

A child's occupation, it is safe to say, is the overcoming of some difficulty. Children are ever active. A man going through all the motions of a youngster on the playground for a day would by night be a worn-out individual. From the random and instinctive movements of infancy the child gradually develops a hierarchy of achievements—sitting, creeping, walking, jumping, balancing, swimming, skating, dancing, gymnastics, physical sports, tricks of contortion, and sleight-of-hand, each the outgrowth of some previous power with a place in the series, each efficient only after persistent practice, each a victory in the child's absorbing struggle for the acquisition of power.

Similarly, play develops the capacity for using tools and for moving objects other than one's own body. Handling is conspicuous in children, as the picking, tearing, lifting, shaking, and throwing movements of the little boy prove. When he leads the dog, the horse, the kite, or his own playmates, he is pursuing the pleasure of being a cause and of extending his own personality. In this process he begins by dropping his playthings and throwing everything helter-skelter. Later he enters into competition to extend his sphere of influence. He learns to project himself by a blow or a throw, as in handball, football, baseball, tennis, golf, croquet, "skipping" pebbles on the water, using a slingshot, shooting a bow and arrow, or firearms. He projects his skill to the behavior of its object. Then there are reciprocal movements, reacting to those of another agent, as in catching, dodging, and parrying. Motor skill, when established, is motor automatism. It comes only through practice, and, in the child, most of practice is play. This play forms an endless chain for the play impulse, as the craving for its satisfaction comes from gradually playing oneself into it.

Curiosity, the prime motive of the childish activity, may assume a destructive or a constructive form. The same analytic instinct of curiosity which moves the child to take things apart or to destroy them for the purpose of seeing what is in them may find a mature development in the interests of the scientific experimenter, the artist, or the philosophic inquirer. The constructive curiosity-play appears in inventions, plans, designs, and the shaping of material in conformity thereto. The sandpile is modeled into mountains, houses, rivers, lakes, beasts and living folk. Collecting represents an allied impulse. The boy's pocket is paralleled only by the girl's trunk. The little urchin who stuffs his pockets with pebbles, bugs, nuts, paper, doughnuts, pennies, or what not, is moved by an impulse related to that which in its more studied and critical form fills our museums, art galleries, and churches.

The higher mental powers normally develop in close connection with the use of the senses and the muscles. Children's games characteristically involve the expression of the whole being; in this lies one of the charms of child play. The child is ever responsive. He is alive to the total environment; and play is the main channel for the free outpouring of his soul in action. His memory is not as yet selective; his remembering is correspondingly indiscriminate. His imagination is not yet schooled; possibilities are not yet distinguished from desires; all he sees is his, the impossible is easy, the easy is impossible, and inanimate nature is animate. He is not yet bound down to systematic thinking in a prescribed channel; his wonder goes out equally to heaven and earth, to his origin and his destiny, to the most trivial details on a par with the riddle of the universe, and his inventions and solutions keep pace with his imagination. His feelings are as yet neither blunted nor refined; he lavishes his tenderest affection upon mud puddles, hobby horses, and cats, as well as upon members of the family; he tortures and abuses the worm, his playmate, or his mother. His instincts have not yet been suppressed; he lives the animal life of his species and is sympathetic with the elemental forces of nature. He is not yet bound to a trade or a profession; his fancy finds expression, his ingenuity is exercised, and his attention is strained, in the effort to copy the patterns of nature, and particularly those set by other human beings. He has not yet developed an organized system of habits; his conscious will is ever free to act out its motives. And in the resulting free action he is strenuous, persistent, indefatigable; he is overcoming difficulties in play.

Growth through play is evident in the development of the social nature of the child, and is especially marked in the development of his consciousness of kinship with a group. The child comes into the world socially inclined, with tendencies toward altruistic as well as toward self-protecting and self-enhancing expressions; but the altruistic nature needs enforcement and direction. Child play reproduces on its level the struggles and achievements of developed social life. Warfare and love, fiendish fight and self-sacrifice, obedience and defiance, the comic and the tragic, regeneration and degeneration, domestic occupation and the spirit of venture —in all these the child lives at his own level, and gradually approaches the stern adult realities, taught and trained, hardened and softened, warmed and cooled, roused and rationalized, through these very engagements in play, which without break or loss of their original character gradually blend into the duties, responsibilities, opportunities, and achievements of adult life.

This conception shows how both mind and body develop more through the exercise of play than through work. Sensory experience gradually acquires associations and responses, comes under control of voluntary attention, and becomes differentiated and serviceable through play; memory, imagination, conception, judgment, and reasoning are whetted, strengthened, and enriched through their exercise in play; the affective life becomes sensitive, adapted, balanced, and serviceable through play; habits are formed, instincts developed, impulses trained and brought under control, streams of subconscious activities crystallized, and the power of attention disciplined through play. In short, play is the principal instrument of growth. It is safe to conclude that, without play, there would be no normal adult cognitive life; without play, no healthful development of affective life; without play, no full development of the power of the will.

Such a statement does not deny the value of work and of tasks deliberately undertaken for immediate ends other than pleasure; it does not deny the place of drudgery, the dull routine, the wearing and tearing obligatory exercise of mind and body; it does not overlook the benefit of the plain every-day work; but it emphasizes the fact that, in mental development as a biological process, spontaneous self-expression, characteristic of play rather than of work, is the larger influence. From the very early years the child should be made to feel the worthiness of being useful, to feel that he has duties of work to perform for himself and for others, thus cultivating a sense of satisfaction in service. Such work sharpens the appetite for play. It is good pedagogy not to make play the avowed object of the childhood days. If the labor is not unduly strenuous, and if it offers sufficient variety of exercise, the useful occupation of the child is better for him than play. The child's occupation should be viewed with reference to the making of a useful individual. Lessons at school should be assigned as work for a definite end; and they should be so regarded by the child. Yet such tasks may well occupy but a portion of his time; the school hours might well be more intensive and shorter than at present. Although the tasks are done for an end in themselves, the activity involves many of the essential elements of the play attitude and play impulses; this is true at least in so far as the child pursues them in a natural way. The tasks well done become a part of a larger play, for the play of life is the child's occupation. He fits himself for life by living it at his own level. The training of play is most effective because, to the player, it is not training, imitation, or pastime, but is part of life. Nature has made the period of infancy and childhood long in order that the fruits of child play might be correspondingly great. It is well for the adult director of the child's activities to realize the largeness of the task of the child; to realize that normal life may be crushed by depriving youth of the rights and opportunities of play; to realize the necessity of encouragement in defeat, of applause in victory, of approval in success, and to exercise sympathetic and prudent selection in shaping the native childish impulses for the making of the man.

PLAY CONTINUES THROUGHOUT NORMAL LIFE

The stimulation of the senses is a source of play. Basking in the sun is a temperature play. Sweetmeats are frequently eaten not for their food value but for the agreeable stimulation of the sense of taste; even bitter and sour substances are played with. Color in nature, in pictures, in dress, and in ornaments is a large part of the source of enjoyment in life; so also is form, both in real objects and as expressed in drawing, painting, sculpture, and architecture. The music lesson may become work, but the artist in music "plays" and reaches his highest mastery through play. The racial development of music and poetry is largely the spontaneous result of play; when genuine and a true expression of impulse, art ever carries the quality of play.

The exercise of memory is a variety of play.

PLAY

The power of reminiscence is one of the charms of life. Primitive man was a story teller. We memorize a great deal for the mere pleasure of memorizing. Recognition gives a feeling of warmth and possession, as in the appreciation of the drama or the interpretation of historical events. The exercise of the imagination is a mental play. The effective novelist lives with his characters. It is the play illusion that makes the writing artistic; and the same spirit is transferred to the reading of fiction and poetry. The theater is by nature as well as by name a playhouse. The imagination invites play, even to the delight of taking liberties with it in the play-effects of the novel, the shocking, the grotesque. Imaginative play constitutes the charm of revery, of mental romance, of musings, and idlings. The child plays with sticks and toys; the adult plays more in images. A score of men engage in action on the football field, while thousands replay the game on the bleachers.

The exercise of the most distinctive mental process, reasoning, may also be play or its close parallel, a game. The guessing of riddles, the flash of wit, the art of conversation, as in the "clash of nothing against nothing," or the systematic encounter of chess are all plays of thought. The emotions enter distinctively into the play of mental

11

life, in that their very presence reflects the enjoyment of the play impulse. Even the despondent misanthrope plays with a morbid craving for bad news, tragedy, and misfortune. Indeed, we enjoy or appreciate most the tragedy that is the truest picture of great misery. If it were not printed on the program that the crucifixion scene in the Passion Play at Oberammergau is a trick illusion, many in the audience would be overwhelmed at the sight of it; yet people travel far for the emotional play which this spectacle represents.

Action is constantly stimulated and directed by the play impulse. The plays of adult life take the form of sport, artistic expression, manifestation of fellowship, and recreation. Sport is the scientific play of the adult. The sportsman has a theory of the game and makes deliberate effort to elaborate and apply it. Hunting, racing, fencing, flying, gambling, etc., are serious and strenuous affairs, carried on with intense interest and application of knowledge, forethought and designed action; yet in so far as they are sports, they are play, first and foremost. Music, poetry, fiction, sketching, painting, and experimenting furnish a most valuable outlet for the loftier sentiments and the creative impulses, enlarging vision, developing feeling, giving form and reality to natural strivings, and conveying ideas from mind to mind in more or less of a play attitude. Dancing, conversation, physical bouts, mental contests, cards, and chess serve the biologically natural purpose of developing a social bond in making man an integral part of the social body—making him something more than a self-centered, self-asserting individual. Fishing, sailing, skating, riding, walking, tennis, cricket, and golf serve as means of recreation, engaging the parts of mind and body that have not been exercised in the labor from which they serve to relieve. Loafing, basking on the beach, bathing in the open water, listening to music, and watching games are forms of rest; they secure equilibrium through the luxury of free abandon to the sway of suggestions, associations, passing imagery, and casual mental occupation.

Adult play, though not to the same extent as child play, is progressive preparation for life. Sport holds its sway only so long as there is room for advancing achievement; one sport follows another in answer to the needs of the maturing man. Plays, like serious occupations and the associations of life, change with the growth of the individual. Recreation, to be effective, must possess an engaging charm in the form of fresh impressions, novel associations, and new outlets for activity. Even rest serves its purpose only in so far as its form is progressively adapted to the changing needs of the constitution. In all these respects play fits for the larger life to the extent that the individual retains plasticity and interest in growth. So long as one is alive, there is ever something to learn. There are visions to be seen, inspirations to be received, ideals to be set aglow, sympathies to be cultivated, emotions to be refined, dreams of achievements to be enjoyed, riddles of life to be solved by the proof of experience. While adult man pursues these objects through systematic efforts and tasks, much of his learning and adaptation for the larger life comes through the exercise of the play impulse and through living in the play attitude. The man or the woman who has ceased to play is to be pitied.

PLAY IS ONE OF THE CHIEF REALIZATIONS OF LIFE

Primitive man lived relatively free from thoughtful care; the child, though endowed with a keen imagination, is disposed to tread in the footsteps of his distant ancestors. Civilization has modified this tendency in two ways: it has established a sense of responsibility, a prudent forethought in the division of labor, and a sympathetic effort to make advancement; on the other hand, it has opened up vast avenues of possibilities, not only for playful expression in art, science, and religion, but also in the increase of means and avenues for pure play. While primitive man was essentially a playing animal, cultured man has vastly more play interests than had his remote ancestor. Indeed, play goes with greatness and with a strenuous life. To Mr. Roosevelt the wilds of Africa and the courts of Europe formed a continuous, fascinating playground in which he played with all his heart, and all his surroundings played their gayest for him while the world proclaimed him a leader in political thought and action.

A vital element in the feeling of self-realization is the experience of growth, not merely consciousness of success in work or play, but the recognition of new power and capacity; it appears in the child's satisfaction in the growth of strength, speed, imagery, thought, and self-control. As there is a conscious satisfaction in knowing the history lesson or the music lesson, so there is a general state of well-being which comes from a sense of equilibrium or adjustment; and this the psychologist traces to the mastery of nature's lessons, which, indeed, are so important that they cannot always be left to the free initiative of the individual, but are provided for by the comprehensive yet compact and ready racial instincts.

Man has an instinct to do everything that he can do. The possession of capacity carries with it the tendency to use that capacity; with the possession of wings goes the tendency to fly, with the possession of the capacity for reflection goes the tendency to reason. Work and the necessities of life develop but a relatively small part of our instinctive resources. Groups of instinctive capacities would be lost were it not for the liberal education of play. It develops those racial traits which have not been called for by the spur of necessity. It elevates even as it levels. Our artificial life is narrow, specialized, and intensive, and this is indeed a condition for great achievements; but play develops the possible man, rather than the man of choice and condition. Dr. Woods Hutchinson says that we are all of about the same age—at least twelve million years. We have been millions of years in the making. Instinct is the conservator of the product of these millions of years, and play is the agent thereof.

The racial life is a reversion to type. When the tired wage-earner comes home from business, he sheds his coat and rolls and romps on the floor—a child with the little children. When vacation comes, we break for forest and stream, mountain and field, and live the simple life. When we join in celebration we shout and sing with abandon. The tendency in play is to fall back upon the elemental. Whatever artifices of war may be devised, fighting plays will always gravitate back toward the simple form of direct bodily contact, be it with fellow-men, beasts, or the forces of nature. It is not plausible to assume that boys climb trees and swim in response to survivals of these specific activities traceable to a distant arboreal or aquatic ancestry. Boys come into this world with limbs fitted for climbing and swimming; trees are common and inviting for climbing, and the water is a great "temptation" to the boy. But the tree and the water challenge curiosity, bravery, and excitement. A strong arm, a well-developed brain for both voluntary and automatic control of that arm, a mental capacity for impulses, images, ideas, and feelings, responsive to the environment—these the child inherits. If free to play, the arm will be put to all manner of tests from the simple and gross to the complex and refined movements. The child appropriates the available. I was telling stories to the children of the neighborhood one evening—stories of my adventures in riding. I told of my riding on elephants, camels, wild bronchos, steers, goats, rams, and dogs. The interest was intense; and to satisfy a last appeal I thought of my first ride and told of a ride on a broomstick. That ended the stories, because the children rushed to find brooms and, for that evening and several days following, the community was invaded by a broomstick cavalry. Had elephants been available, elephant rides would have been preferred, because they were more imposing.

The realization of a sense of freedom is an essential and distinctive trait of play. Witness the plays of freedom in movement, imagination, and choice. In the very desire for mastery freedom is the goal. With power, as with duty, come restriction and strain to millionaire, ruler, or servant. He, therefore, turns to play for diversion, and for the expression of his heart cravings. Whether in sport, art, invention, adventure, social contact, recreation, or rest, the sense of freedom which play generates is an enduring value.

Play attracts, engages, and fascinates by the very satisfaction which it engenders and which supports it. The dance, when it is real play and not mere social labor or conformity, carries the dancer away, in so far as he falls into a state of diffuse and dreamy consciousness, intoxicated by the sense of pleasure, lulled by the automatic rhythmic movements, and soothed by the melodious and measured flow of the music. This element of ardent fascination or elation with mental intoxication may be seen in some degree in all play—in the romping of the infant, the adolescent mating plays, the sport and adventure of youth, or the recreation of the adult. Indeed, in this fascination lies a grave danger of play—the danger of overindulgence.

The satisfaction in being a cause is one of the compelling motives to play as well as one of its direct rewards. Closely related to this is the feeling of extension of personality. This is well illustrated in games of competition. The boy who flies the kite the highest is the champion of the group. He who in the flash of wit parries best and thrusts most keenly is master for the moment. The adventurer is the hero in proportion to his success in thrilling deeds. In so far as achievement expresses and reflects our freest ambition, fancy, or ideals, it is rated as a part of ourselves, of our cherished personalities.

Play is essentially social; it is, therefore, natural that one of its aims and rewards should be a sense of fellowship. Laying aside petty differences, interests, and points of vantage, the playing group fuses into a common consciousness on a plane of equality, with common means, common interests, and common enjoyments. Play is the making of social man. It is that which welds the bonds of fellowship in the social group. We become like those with whom we play. A sense of fellowship with those whom we cherish is one of the truest rewards of life.

Play is satisfying because it is positive, even aggressive. It stands for acquisition, seriousness, and optimism, as may be observed in a comparison of the child that is busy at play with the child that does not play, or the adult who is young at heart and finds self-expression in play with the youth who has lost this plasticity. Strong proof of this is found in the fact that the feeble-minded play comparatively little.

Play is an expression of the joy of life. This joy is expressed most characteristically not so much in deliberate, systematic play as in the entry of the play attitude in work, or its reflection in nature, truth, and other stern realities. Indeed, everything in life presents aspects of play to the eyes of the mentally alert. The play attitude is the most universal medium for the manifestation of a sense of freedom and conviction of the worth of life when these exist.

The unrestraint and spontaneity of play result in a strenuous and whole-hearted exertion. When we work, we walk or plod; when we play, we skip or run. When performing a duty, we do as much as is required; but when we play, we do all we can. Work seldom leads to overdoing, but play offers great temptation in that direction. If football players worked as hard at their mental tasks as on the football field, there would be fewer failures in the classroom. If every child grew up to work as hard as he plays, it would be necessary to form more unions to limit the hours of labor. Extreme exertion attracts, especially when it is irresistible and joyous as in play.

The seriousness of play is one of its fascinations. If we join in a game and are not serious or zealous about it, we are not playing. To play means to be in the game. It is engrossing absorption that drives dull care away. It is not the little golf ball but its zealous pursuit that compels the attention of mature men to the complete exclusion of business and professional cares.

The final secret of the success of play is its fictitious nature; it rests upon make-believe. Liberated from realities, it accepts the ideal and lives it as real. Each game has its distinctive charm. There is the attraction of variety in the very choice of games, in changes from day to day and from season to season, and in a progressive order from one game to another.

The moments of supreme satisfaction, the moments of highest realization and appreciation of life come from activities which are most conspicuously characterized by play attitudes—either from play pure and simple, or from work in which play-motives dominate. We all have our work, our set tasks and duties; but those of us who get the most out of life are they whose work would be their preferred play, quite apart from its pursuit as a means of livelihood. Conversely, the truest and most fortunate are those who obtain their relaxation, rest, recreation, stimulation, and self-expression without making tasks of them. The things we do for the pleasure of doing are the rewards of life; they are an expression of the freed self, the channels of release from the routine of necessity, the sources of inspiration, power, and satisfaction.

THE PLAY IMPULSE AND THE PLAY ATTITUDE ARE DISTINCTIVE TRAITS OF RELIGION

The function of play is to prepare for life, to enhance life, and to furnish a medium for self-realization. To illustrate these three purposes in a specific relation, the rôle of play in religion—a realm with which we are not accustomed to associate play

—may be selected. If it can be shown that play holds an important place in such an apparently distant field, its rôle in more generally recognized relations, such as art, education, commerce, and medicine, will be more firmly established.

We are accustomed to regard play as an outlet for surplus energy, as a life of semblance and sham in contrast with serious work and reverent worship, as something to be avoided when we engage in religious exercises; but, from our present view, play is a preparation for religious life, and is one of the chief means of its realization.

In the foregoing we have found that among the most salient traits of play are a self-realization through growth, a conservation of the racial inheritance, a sense of freedom, a thrill of elation or fascination, an extension of personality, a bond of fellowship, a positive-mindedness, a passive seriousness, an exhibition of joy in life, and an indulgence in make-believe. We must now inquire to what extent these play traits are characteristic of religion.

Religious ceremony has its origins close to those of play; and religion has invariably been linked with ceremonials. The Book of Psalms, which is one of the most sturdy and virile expressions of religious consciousness, teems with exhortations to sing, shout, make a loud noise, play, and dance to the glory of the Lord. While crude ceremonials are conspicuous in primitive religion, the same play elements continue in a refined form in progressively evolving higher forms of religion. Indeed, the highest type of religion is that which is characterized by the noble play attitude. Mass is celebrated; celebration, from the singing of the gospel hymns to the rendition of the sacred oratorio, is an expression of the play-motif of freedom, exultation, and faith.

Religion is a growth; it is a preparation for a larger life. The growth which religion implies comes through exercise. The labored, set, necessary exercise produces a servile, negative, and stale religion; the religion of love, happiness, and faith grows through spontaneous self-expression for the love of expression. There is nothing more mysterious about this growth than about any other mental growth. Religious sensibility, religious discernment, religious ideas, religious emotions, religious habits, the religious self-surrender, all grow through the progressive exercise of these various capacities, in religion as well as out of religion. The sentiment of gratitude to God grows to a higher stature through the spontaneous reaction to the vision of divine goodness by which the soul is set aglow than through a set expression of gratitude as a matter of duty. So repentance is not so much an obligatory affair as the free and irresistible expression resulting from a progressive change in point of view.

While play preserves the racial inheritance and develops the whole man, this end is a specific aim of religion. Religious life is instinctive. We are religious because we are religious organisms. We are born with a craving for self-realization along all lines of development, and this craving satisfies itself largely through play. For this reason religion is largely emotional, and emotion is conservative of the non-rationalized issues of heredity and environment.

The sense of freedom is prominent in religious life—the self-expression of the soul set free. We play when we are free; religion has always been a breaking away from the bonds and cares of this world. "Consider the lilies of the field; they toil not, neither do they spin." We play when we have opportunity for rest; religion has always been associated with rest, which, by the way, often means change of occupation. The Sabbath was established as a religious institution. We play when we are in need of recreation; religion is not only a haven of rest but a fountain for the renewal of life's energies. The freedom which in ordinary play comes from a sense of freedom in movement is limited in comparison with that freedom which comes to the devout in taking hold of the Infinite by faith.

Fascination, or a sense of elation, characterizes religious life. Religious devotion, religious faith, religious fervor, from that of the ignorant and credulous to that of the inspired seer and savant, reveal this trait. The history of conversion, revivals, and great religious movements corroborates this view. Religious heroism and religious serenity as well as religious fanaticism picture it. The transcendent joy of the sane and cultured devout man reveals it in its noblest form. In all ages religion has had devices for cultivating this sense of fascination and elation.

The feeling of extension of personality finds its fullest expression in the religious attitude. That communion with the Infinite which comes over one who worships in nature is a reaching out into the larger spiritual self. The "new person" that comes through regeneration measures its relation to the world in entirely new terms. Faith is power; in a very real sense we are what we believe ourselves to be.

Many of our religious conceptions are based on the idea of a fellowship-attitude such as the fatherhood of God, the brotherhood of mankind, the sacrifice of love, abounding grace, and the joy and comfort in spiritual inheritance. Christian fellowship is the supreme test of religion. Social life in the church is a fellowship. Church dinners serve other purposes than that of raising funds. The institutional church operates not only for economic results, but primarily for the development of the religious life. The kindergarten in Sunday schools is a most serviceable form of religious instruction for young children. Boys' military societies, students' receptions, and pastors' calls serve to build up fellowship. But to force entertainment upon the youth does not develop the play-attitude. It is not the entertainment, but the genuine self-expression that develops fellowship. It is not amusement and having things done for us, but the feeling of responsibility and opportunity for playing our part with a free hand and a warm heart, that develops fellowship.

We may divide religions into negative and positive; or into the religion of self-denial and the religion of self-expression and joy. In the progressively higher and higher forms of religion we find, as in play, more of this positive element which is the sign of natural self-expression.

The lives of the saints have been a mystery to the non-religious. The equanimity, joy, and even triumph which they have shown in the face of apparent suffering, discouragement, obstacles, and grief is one of the wonders of the human spirit. Devotion makes play of work; it makes torture pleasure; and it makes faith the beginning of life. One side of religion is represented by self-abasement, humiliation, confession, and petition; another by self-assertion in praise, thanksgiving, and adoration. Each has its place, but the argument of play emphasizes the latter.

Religion in its demand for serious exertion requires the efficiency of a spontaneous interest. Only the instinctive, spontaneous, and natural impulse could bring about the self-assertion of religious devotion. This idea of whole-souled self-expression harmonizes with the sacred nature of religious exercises. There is nothing greater in social man than love; but by the very fact of its greatness and worth it is one of the commonest objects of play. The same principle applies to our reactions to divine love. The fact that there is a serious and solemn attitude does not deprive the exercise of the character of play. All sport is serious.

The play object is often the most real and serviceable. One morning my little boy said, "Jack Frost has made pretty figures on the windows." Jack Frost is avowedly a play conception and we grown-ups tend to treat it with an air of superiority; but no student of meteorology and the metaphysics of matter and force can tell us in final terms what puts the frost figures upon the window. As we advance in knowledge we go farther and farther back, merely to fit the level of our intellectual grasp, but to this day we have only gone a few steps in the infinite regression of retreats. One is safe in saying, "Tell me what the frost is and I will tell you what God is." All we have is merely more or less serviceable symbols for the reality of matter as well as for the conception of God. In a recent sermon the minister preached on the question, "What is God?" and showed that God had at sundry times been identified with graven images, the forces of nature, and a big physical man on a throne. "All these," he said, "are low and unworthy conceptions. I will tell you what God is. God is love." The congregation felt warmed up and satisfied with the final solution. But, alas! though the conception of God as a big man is anthropomorphic, that of God as love is also an anthropomorphism. Man and love are mere symbols upon which our minds rest in the ever on-going struggles toward the conception of the infinite. "God is a loving father" is a serviceable conception only because the mind is willing to rest itself in the play attitude.

Now, the fact that fellowship, for example, is present in both play and religion does not prove that play is present in all religion, nor that religion is present in all play. But when we take ten or more of the most salient features of play, as we have done, and find that these are among the most salient features of religious life, then there is some reason for saying that there is a relationship.

Our picture has been drawn from the point of view that play represents a characteristic attitude of mind, a phase of which we find in religion. But, observe also the obverse view, that religion is present in play. We feel more religious when we play golf, sail, climb mountains, or bask in the sun than when held down to our fixed tasks of work. Religion is affiliated with play, in that play implies the launching of oneself upon the elevating forces in life; it represents an attitude of well-being and surrender to the beneficent forces of nature.

As life develops and becomes more intellectualized, spiritualized, and refined in its sentiments the play attitude matures into the more serious types of self-expression. Quiet worship, contemplation, teaching, and ministration become the equivalent, in the developed soul, of games in the undeveloped.

The attitude is similar; a parallel purpose is served; kindred instincts operate; there is simply an adaptation of the self-expression to the stage of development.

Briefly, the attitudes and experiences which we call play characterize a very large part of our religious experience; the religion of daily life shows itself most naturally in the moments of free self-expression for the pleasure of expression.

Upon first impression the point of view thus urged may seem to lower the dignity of religion, to imply doubtful sanction of morality and a skeptical questioning about the possibility of knowledge; but such fears are ill founded. Serious study of the rôle of play in religion reveals the vital factor of natural self-expression with reference to a non-rationalized sanction of goodness; it leads to a serene appreciation of the spiritual self; it lays a cornerstone in the foundation of our religious pedagogy.

PSYCHOLOGY ANALYZES, DESCRIBES AND EXPLAINS PLAY

Our survey has served to show that play has a place in daily life at once interesting, significant, and vitally practical. It is the business of psychology to analyze, describe, and explain play as a mental activity. The first step in the psychological analysis of play is to secure the data for its classification, both as impulses and as results. The features of play must be reduced to their elements, yielding such factors as spontaneous expression of joy, a feeling of the extension of personality, and the attitude of make-believe. Upon this basis unrecognized varieties and aspects of play may be identified, and factors which do not comply with the adopted criteria may be eliminated.

What classification we shall make depends upon what purpose it is to serve. We may classify the people of a city according to location of residence, occupation, bank-rating, education, church and club affiliations, social standing, sex, age, color, height, etc. Any one classification may be as true and as serviceable as another. Similarly in play, an internal classification may emphasize the psychological relations of instinctive tendencies, impulses, sensory processes, ideational elements, motor forms, etc.; while the external classification regards plays as units, distinguishing them according to the purpose served, the motive present, the order of evolution, the dominant aspect, the relation to other activities, to age, sex, temperament, and occupation of the player. Such a description through classification of play and plays is the foundation for the answer to the question, "What is play?"

The psychology of play indicates that play is not a single, simple, unmixed, unrelated activity of life; it is larger in scope, more vital in function, deeper in significance than is commonly recognized. The provisional definition of play as a free self-expression for the pleasure of expression is manifestly too broad, even though it be interpreted to include Ruskin's limitation, "and with no determined end." Just how play is to be differentiated from other activities of the same general sort is not as yet clear. "Work" and "play" are inadequate terms to indicate all the included activities. Likewise is it true that work and play blend by infinite gradations, that what is work to one is play to another, that what is play to one at one time is not play at another time, that from one point of view a given act is play while from another it is work, and that in normal life the two are intimately blended. In all favorable occupations much that goes by the name of work is done in the spirit of play; and, conversely, much that goes by the name of play is downright drudgery. Witness many of the "social duties" which have the appearance of play but are often done as painful tasks. The greater part of life is neither wholly play nor wholly work. The scientific study of play will substitute a large number of specific terms for the vague term, "play," as has been done in the case of the term "memory." We now speak of impression, retention, association, recall, recognition, and redintegration, etc., and thereby designate specific features of the memory process, each of which may occur in processes other than memory. There need, therefore, be no dispute in the future as to what is work and what is play, for discussion will center upon the analysis, description, and explanation of specific instincts, impulses, associations, attitudes, and actions characteristic of play, regardless of whether they occur in play or in other activity.

The explanation of play involves (1) a general picture of the process, (2) the physiological correlations and conditions, (3) the motives present, (4) the origin and mode of development, and (5) the biological purpose. To illustrate in the case of one of these factors, say the third, in a specific type of play activity, we ask, for example, what is it that moves the child to babble in rhythmic jingles and adult man to scan in poetic measure? Aside from content, considering form only and excluding rhyme, we find that one of the many motives present is the inherent pleasure in rhythm. What, then, is the nature of the pleasure in rhythm? Rhythm favors perception by grouping; rhythm adjusts the strain of attention; rhythm produces a feeling of balance; rhythm gives a sense of freedom and luxury; rhythm gives a feeling of power—it carries; rhythm gives a stimulating and a lulling effect indicative of an inceptive elation and ecstasy; rhythm is one of the well-nigh universal periodicities of nature which we instinctively crave; rhythm finds resonance in the whole organism; rhythm makes use of violence and novelty; rhythm arouses balanced movements, or images of such movements; rhythm arouses and sustains enriching associations. But why and how does each of these factors contribute toward the pleasureableness of rhythm? Why, to take the first only, does favorable perception through grouping give pleasure? It uses the most effective form of attention, the secondary passive form; it utilizes the attention-wave at its maximum crest; it enables us to know how much is coming; it places unusual emphasis upon words; it throws us into the artistic attitude. But why is the secondary passive form of attention so agreeable? Among other things, because it is purposive and passive. And why is the purposive and passive so agreeable? Among other things, because it is effective and easy. And why is the effective and easy so agreeable? Among other things, because human nature craves the largest returns from a minimum outlay. And why does human nature crave this? Because it tends to preserve life.

We should not take alarm at the looming up of the magnitude of this task, for play occurs in accord with mental laws; a general knowledge of the laws of mental life facilitates the explanation. The vital thing for us to seek, if we would have a true perspective of play, is not narrow knowledge of play in itself and apart from other expressions of our nature, but rather knowledge of the general laws of mental life, the power of psychological insight, that will relate the psychology of play to the psychology of man. A botanist knows more about a plant upon first seeing it than the tyro who has closely examined it without a general knowledge of botany.

A more complete explanation of any particular speech-rhythm play would involve an account of its component mental elements, a recognition of their physiological correlates, of the motives which may be considered to be the cause of the play, the evolution thereof, the recognition of its immediate end, and the biological purposes which it serves for the individual and society. For practical purposes the explanation may be reduced to the naming of the features or processes composing the acts as understood. Thus, assuming that the nature of the pleasurableness of rhythmic sound is known, "the pleasure of rhythm" becomes a pertinent explanation.

The study of the psychology of play thus contributes much to the systematic survey of the facts of mind in our daily activities; it adds to the general hold upon life in power of interpretation which is a part of culture; it indicates at least the general direction in which efficiency, through the control of natural sources, lies; it adds to the appreciation of the origin, the complexity, and the beauty of mental nature; it provides in part a basis for our more philosophical means and purposes; it gives an enlarged and more intimate meaning to the relation of the sciences that deal with physical nature to those that deal with mind; it furnishes a basis for application to the arts of conduct in the crafts, in education, in right living. It is therefore meet that the psychology of play should serve as an introduction and a contribution to the "psychology of daily life."

CHAPTER II

SERVICEABLE MEMORY

President Porter said that a good memory depends upon a good digestion, a good logic, and a good conscience. Health, the power of mental application, and an upright life—these are the fundamental conditions of good memory. We may take for granted the first and the last of these conditions, which come within the domain of physiology and ethics respectively, and consider the psychological factor of mental economy.

A good memory is not one that remembers everything. If one were doomed to remember everything that came within his experience, he would find himself hopelessly swamped, distracted, possibly insane. Certain forms of idiocy present an allied lack of organization.

The test of a good memory is that it shall be serviceable; that the mind shall be furnished and ready with just the sort of facts which may be needed, and free from the encumbrances of useless, irrelevant, or distracting material. In addition, these facts should be accurate, "faithful to the original"; they should be long retained, if necessary; they should come promptly, easily, and conveniently. Improvement in memory will be judged with reference to these and allied standards.

A valuable body of knowledge in regard to the nature of the memory process and the principle of acquisition has been accumulated by experimental methods. Instead of summarizing these facts in a technical way I shall formulate a series of simple rules of memory-training in the language of everyday experience, in so far as possible, in harmony with these facts. The chief statements will be put in the form of commands or rules; not for the sake of exhortation, let it be emphatically said, but for the sake of clearness and brevity.

These rules may be grouped under four general heads: Impression, Association, Recall, and Recognition. Under these only the more typical rules are considered; details or qualifications must be omitted. This is not a memory "system"; it is merely a series of selected illustrations. The artifice of a "corollary" under each rule is not taken in a rigid, logical sense, but merely serves to suggest, through a single illustration, something of the rich radiations of a given rule.

PSYCHOLOGY IN DAILY LIFE

I. RULES OF IMPRESSION

1. *Select Your Field of Interest.* (Selection).
Corollary: Dare to be ignorant of many things.

Nature provides for rigid selection in all directions by setting limits to our capacities, thereby forcing instinctive selection of interests and favoring the formation of ruts. We may, however, vastly enhance the serviceableness of our memory by a deliberate selecting of life interests which we shall take seriously by our nature and choice as well as by the force of circumstances. To remember serviceably is to reach promptly the data desired; and, to do this systematically, the mind's eye must be trained to focus automatically upon the desired memory-object.

If one is to be a banker he should train himself actively and systematically to remember facts pertaining to banking: not that he should limit his interests to banking; he must have life interests, such, for example, as pertain to social life, to health, or to intellectual pursuits. But these interests should be only a few out of the many toward which he might be inclined by nature. It is the man who keeps his mind on banking during banking hours who becomes a financier. If he attends in the same way to other obligations out of banking hours he will be also socially attractive and will find satisfaction in a larger life. This is true alike in the humbler walks of life and in its highest pursuits.

Occasional and casual selection of memory-objects does not strengthen memory power, but on the contrary often weakens it. To strengthen memory the selection must follow a system of habits based upon life interests. This implies that the selection shall be made in large units of interest; that intruding interests shall be eliminated by habits of application; that the mind, free from anxiety, shall feel itself adjusted to the situations which confront it.

2. *Intend to Remember* (Intention).
Corollary: Trust your memory.

An Indian woman began her business career by trading in primitive fashion with the pioneers in a village of Colorado. The population grew gradually, and with it her trade expanded into a large general merchandise establishment which supplied the community with everything from food, clothing, and jewelry to threshing-machines. This woman remained her own bookkeeper. She maintained an extensive credit account, but kept no books. She trusted her memory; and it served her well because the demands upon it increased so gradually that she never lost confidence in herself.

To intend to remember means to fix the impression with confidence. To trust memory means to have the habit of intending to remember. Sporadic intentions are unreliable. The intentions that count in life are habitual—constant, not casual. When the intention to remember has become a habit, memory serves with little effort; instead of being a matter of concern, remembering becomes a matter of comfort and ease, just as does truth telling. Such is the natural habit of a good memory. We enjoy things, we observe distinctions, we think truths, trusting that they are ours; and our memory serves us well.

3. *Attend to the Selected Object* (Attention).
Corollary: Secure the most effective form of attention.

Put yourself into such a channel of life that what you need to remember is that in which you are naturally interested.

The majority of college students who are unfit for study might be discovered by this criterion: "Has this student a natural interest in that which he is trying to learn?" College authorities might do well to apply this test rigidly early in the course and eliminate those who find no natural interest in their studies, thereby encouraging them before too late to seek other channels of education in which they would find themselves effectual. The charge to the entering freshman should be: "Learn that which you care for; and, if the college course does not arouse in you a feeling of fitness for the work, go elsewhere; for there is something wrong either with you or with the college."

Our rule is, therefore, not the trite admonition: "Pay attention." That rule has its value; but voluntary attention is seldom more than a precarious makeshift in the ordinary work and experiences of life; it is too rare and costly. Voluntary attention is one of the highest and most indispensable achievements of man, but the attention that serves the steady flow of the stream of consciousness must be spontaneous and yet semi-automatic. It may be called derived primary attention because it has been favored and encouraged until it has become second nature. Attention to a dog fight is passive, but attention to the traits and achievements of dogs from the point of view of the dog-fancier or of the animal psychologist is secondary passive, because it flows from a consciously directed natural interest.

This rule affects the entire plan of our daily life. Power depends upon leverage. In memory, as in all other forms of force, the main thing is to get a leverage; and the best leverage for memory is a genuine interest. The modern movement in vocational direction will do much to increase the serviceableness of the memory-grasp of those who are wisely guided into natural channels of life-work.

4. *Grasp the Elements* (Elements).

Corollary: Let essentials stand out in relief.

To remember the above three rules after they have been understood it is not necessary to fix the more than five hundred words comprised in the statements and illustrations. A single key-word for each rule will suffice; for example, selection, intention, attention. To impress the illustrations and interpretations in their elements the mental note might run something like this:

Selection: nature's selection, banker, habit;

Intention: squaw, habit;

Attention: studies, derived primary, leverage.

The key-word for each rule must represent a concrete unit of thought; and the three key-words for the respective rules must be grasped as a single unit embodying the common element of the three ideas—namely, concentration upon the impression.

SERVICEABLE MEMORY

The good reader will have analyzed in this way, because it is his way of reading, and at this point the thought stands out concrete and logical; whereas the inferior reader will have "plowed through the stuff" in a helpless way and cannot retrace his steps, because he has not grasped the elements in the reading. The effect of observing and of thinking in terms of the elements involved is not merely to reduce the number of necessary words or symbols, but rather to give perspective to the essentials. It affords something to take hold of, a hook whereon to hang the mental belongings.

5. *Trust the Primary Impression* (Primacy).
Corollary: Master as you go.

The facts relating to the attention wave, and the proper mastery of elements, as described above, have a striking application here. If you want a good, clear picture by time exposure take one exposure of the required length. Do not blur by trying to get a summation of impressions. So, in making a mental picture, observe so as to grasp the object in a single firm impression. Trust that impression and seal it with the intention to remember.

This principle is opposed to the rote method. To memorize a poem do not merely grind it over and over in a mechanical way, but, after a preliminary reading, read it logically; go slowly, step by step, intending to learn it in the best way; attend to the task with a mind prepared to discover the essential elements of the structure and determined to make the first impression trustworthy.

The rules of memory may be represented by a pyramid; the side of the pyramid, which we have now approached, is designated Impression. Reading from the base upward, the steps or elevations rise in this natural order:

Primacy: Trust the primary impression
Elements: Grasp the elements
Attention: Attend to the selected object
Intention: Intend to remember
Selection: Select your field of interest

6. *Practice Systematic Impression* (Practice).
Corollary: "Do it now."

Ordinarily the development of memory is left to chance, to a casual issue. We know only a few of the laws of memory and make but little effort to apply these. We grow up so gradually that there is ordinarily no particular moment at which the value of practice is forced upon us. In the training of the young there might well be introduced some instruction in the principles of memory training, to be followed by a régime in which the command, "Do it now," could be enforced. Systematic training yields remarkable results, whether the memory be originally very good or only ordinarily retentive. It is not necessary to set drill exercises on mere drill material, nor is it necessary or desirable to follow any of the hundreds of artificial systems sold by professional trainers of memory. The thing to do is to learn the fundamental facts about memory and then simply apply them as we go about our ordinary duties of the day. Practice in the right way the impression of the facts that you need from day to day. No more economic lesson could be set than to learn by doing the very thing you are to do. Meet the situations which are a part of your life routine with the habits of interest, trust, discernment, thought, and application and you will practice the above six rules and many others with a corresponding growth in efficiency. Crown the pyramid of Impression, then, by the capstone, Practice.

II. RULES OF ASSOCIATION

1. *Recognize Relationships* (Relationships).
Corollary: Be familiar with the laws of association.

PSYCHOLOGY IN DAILY LIFE

It is announced that a friend is to be married in June. The moment I hear this I say to myself: "How appropriate! June is the wedding month; it is the month of roses; it is the month which symbolizes the blossoming into life. I cannot fail to remember it." In this way we ordinarily relate impressions, be they ever so isolated or abstract.

Our rule does not imply any one formulated application of association but rather the habitual attitude of appreciation. But this power of appreciation is vastly increased and strengthened by insight into the nature of the laws of association. Despite their controversial history among psychologists, the rules of association are in fact surprisingly few and clear to common sense.

Our rule is to observe the relations of impressions. Knowledge of these possible relations facilitates the presentation of facts, and supplies us a means of holding them for recall. One illustration must suffice. The law of similarity is the basis of all scientific classification; without it there could be no science. The botanist can recognize and recall thousands of plants because he has formed the habit of seeing relationships. One plant is like another plant in this, and that, and another respect; therefore they belong to the same class. Instead of remembering the hundred or thousand individual

48

plants, the botanist remembers only one representative plant and the relationships within the class to which it belongs. This is often pictured in a more or less composite image; but the consciousness involved in that image is the consciousness of relations. Our first rule of association is the general charge to equip the mind with knowledge about the nature and significance of association. Set your facts in a system of relations.

2. *Form Habits of Analyzing* (Analysis).
Corollary: Learn by thinking.

This rule may be variously illustrated. It is a favorite principle in the modern mnemonic systems of which the system of Loisette is a good illustration. Loisette was a famous memory teacher in New York. The main secret of his system (and it was sold as a secret) consisted in a somewhat artificial application of this principle. Taking the three laws of association which he called inclusion, exclusion, and concurrence, he devised a progressive series of exercises in which the learner acquired great ability in discovering clear-cut relations, *i.e.,* the ability to perceive and recall in terms of such relations consciously recognized, yet directly and easily as one sees directly and without effort the color of a flower. The following is his illustration of the meaning of the first law, inclusion:

INCLUSION indicates that there is an *overlapping* of *meaning* between two words, or that there is a *prominent idea* or *sound* that belongs to both alike, or that a similar fact or property belongs to two events or things as, to enumerate a few classes:

Whole and Part.—(Earth, Poles.) (Ship, Rudder.) (Forest, Trees.) (Air, Oxygen.) (House, Parlor.) (Clock, Pendulum.) (Knife, Blade.) (India, Punjab.) (14, 7.) (24, 12.)

Genus and Species.—(Animal, Man.) (Plant, Thyme.) (Fish, Salmon.) (Tree, Oak.) (Game, Pheasant.) (Dog, Retriever.) (Universal Evolution, Natural Selection.) (Silver Lining, Relief of Lucknow.) (Empress, Queen Victoria.) (Money, Cash.)

Abstract and Concrete.—(The same Quality appears both in the Adjective and in the Substantive.)—(Dough, Soft.) (Empty, Drum.) (Lion, Strong.) (Eagle, Swift.) (Courage, Hero.) (Glass, Smoothness.) (Gold, Ductility.) (Sunshine, Light.) (Fire, Warmth.)

Similarity of Sound.—(Emperor, Empty.) (Salvation, Salamander.) (Hallelujah, Hallucination.) (Cat, Catastrophe.) (Top, Topsy.)

SERVICEABLE MEMORY

Simple Inclusion embraces cases not found in either of the foregoing classes, but where there is *something in common* between the pairs, as (Church, Temple.) (Pocket, Black Hole.)

The first exercise consists in learning the following list of ten words in a single reading by aid of the recognition of these principles of inclusion:

Building
Dwelling } Genus and Species.

Dwelling
House } Synonyms.

House
Parlor } Whole and Part.

Parlor
Partridge } Similarity by Sight and Sound.

Partridge
Feathers } Whole and Part.

Feathers
Light } Concrete and Abstract.

Light
Lighterman } Sight and Sound.

Lighterman
Lord Mansfield $\Big\}$ Sight and Sound.

Lord Mansfield
Field hand $\Big\}$ Sight and Sound.

Such analysis of the words and their relations serves to fix the relationship, and it is possible to repeat the list forward and backward after one such reading. Applying this principle to the remembering of numbers, Loisette gives such illustrations as these: the height of Pike's Peak is 14,147 feet; observe that the number consists of two 14s and a half of 14. Fusiyama, the noted volcano of Japan, is 12,365 feet high; observe that this number is made up of the number of months and of days in the year—12 and 365.

This may serve as a partial illustration of a memory system which possesses some merit. As a matter of fact, now that it is printed in a book and sold for a dollar, very little use is made of it. When it was sold for fifty dollars or more, with a pledge of secrecy, the buyer actually followed the directions in order to get what he paid for; and he often got it. Merely to read the book will be of no avail. If there were some contrivance by which one could extract fifty dollars for the chapter on memory training which you are now reading, its usefulness would be greatly increased.

3. *Force Concrete Imagery* (Forcing).
Corollary: Fix the first fancy.

By following this rule a person with ordinary memory may learn a list of fifty or a hundred disconnected words in a single reading so that he can repeat the whole list either forward or backward. Try it. Here are the instructions: Have some one read a list of words slowly, or uncover one word at a time by yourself, and at the very first impression that you get from the words observe some connection (the more bizarre the better) between the new word and the preceding one; picture this relationship concretely and add a new section to the group image for each new word added to the chain of words; fix the first fancy of each relationship, and image it boldly. But before we try the experiment let us illustrate the procedure with a short list of words.

Boy—I see a little barefooted boy
Grass—walking in the tall grass;
Glass—the stalks of grass crackle like glass under his feet:

Pike—therefore he is glad when he sees the open pike,

   Scissors—his little legs clip like scissors,

   Ventilation—and his lungs get good ventilation,

   Bird—for he flies like a bird

   Nickel—and swings his nickel-plated rod

   Fury—like fury

   Gear—because he is now in gear with nature.

Each learner will have a different set of associations. It is important that he should use his own, and, so far as possible, use the first association that comes to his mind. It is the concrete imaging of the fancied situations as a unit that welds the words together in memory.

As a matter of fact, this is the method we naturally employ in ordinary routine memory. There is an automobile accident, and a witness is called to report. He can give a fairly good report because he has a definite notion of the relations of figures in the scene: the chauffeur looking back, the horse struck on the front knees, the lady's hatpin flying in the air, the first aid to the injured, horses and rider, etc.

4. *Grasp in Large Units* (Large Units).
Corollary: Remember ideas, not words.

In one sense memory improves with **mental**

growth because we learn to think in larger and larger units. A little boy goes with his father to a museum and sees a collection of shells. The boy sees and will remember a few forms which strike his fancy, but the father who knows his systematic classification is able to give a better account of the group, for he learned by large units, whereas the boy treated each shell as an individual object, with the exception possibly of obvious similarities.

5. *Observe Synthetically* (Synthesis).
Corollary: Build elements into a whole.

This rule is a rule of accumulation. In reading for the purpose of memorizing the proper procedure is to read each word in the sentence and, before proceeding further, to grasp the sentence as a unit; then, treating the sentence as an element in the same way, to grasp the paragraph as a unit of sentences.

To bind the impression once firmly grasped be familiar with the bonds that fasten new acquisitions to what you already have, examine these ties deliberately and make sure that they bind; clinch with some additional ties—the first that you find in your own rich personal supply; make each bundle as large as you can, and then tie all the bundles together.

Here, then, is a second side of our pyramid, Association: (Observe the steps in order from below.)

Synthesis: Observe synthetically
Large units: Grasp in large units
Forcing: Force concrete imagery
Analysis: Form habits of analyzing
Relationships: Recognize relationships

6. *Practice*.

As in impression, so in association, knowledge of these laws is of no use unless it be put into practice. In itself, the knowledge is not power. One trial does not give power. The power of association is fully effective only when it is so firmly ingrained by practice as to operate automatically and irresistibly, and therefore with ease. Mounting the pyramid from the side of Association, we rise from another side to the original capstone, Practice.

III. RULES OF RECALL

1. *Be Persistent in the Effort to Recall* (Persistence).

Corollary: Seek clues and follow them: try.

This is the logical sequel to the rule of impression, "Intend to remember." It is a very common occurrence that we have established good impressions in association and yet fail through negligence in the recall. If the memory image is not at command as soon as sought we all too readily conclude that we cannot reach it.

Ability to recall is not, like the ability to lift or the ability to hear, restricted by any sharply limiting sense organ. If the memory image comes to me immediately, that is largely a matter of chance; I chance to have in mind the impression or idea which has such associations with the image sought that it draws it out promptly. Our rule encourages us to use all our effort and ingenuity in search for an association which shall draw out the desired image. Mere blind persistence, often the mere lapse of time, brings out the proper association; but vastly more can be accomplished if the effort is made to review systematically the events which lead up to the desired link. We must retrieve, not merely flush, the game.

Here again the importance does not attach so much to the isolated effort as to the formation of the habit of discovering clues and following them. Training in this will place at one's command a power of insight into relations and a power to follow lines of association tenaciously, yet without effort.

2. *Repeat the Recall Often* (Repetition).

Corollary: Never miss the opportunity of seeing a good friend.

It has been said that to learn a technical subject, such as anatomy, one must have forgotten it several times and have learned it over again. That is what happens as a rule in our casual occupations, but it is very wasteful. The more economic way is to trust the initial impression; hold it until it is fixed by some bond of association; then, instead of repeating the impression, recall and repeat the recall as often as may be necessary. One recall is worth more than a dozen impressions because it is the recall and not the impression which we aim to fix.

This rule has two distinct applications. In the first place, it gives us the procedure for the building up of a complex impression, such as a long definition or a poem. As we have seen above, the impressions should be cumulative; that is, the reader should learn one after another the elements of the impression singly or in simple groups, and then progressively unite these until the complex is grasped as a whole. In the welding together of these elements in the impression the elements should be handled in recall, and not in repeated impressions of parts. Thus the impression in the case of a complete memory object passes gradually by steps from impression to recall, and the impression is not complete until the large units can be held firm and true in clear recall.

In the second place, the rule applies to the securing of permanent retention. Instead of forgetting the anatomy and then going back to learn it over and over again, the economic way is to review in memory, instead of in impression, as often as may be necessary to prevent the intrusion of errors in recall. There are, of course, exceptions to this rule. I learn the streets of a city for guidance on a visit, but if I am not to visit that city for twenty years it would be waste of energy to keep that memory alive. The rule applies, however, to all cases in which we desire to keep the remembrance continuously available.

3. *Be Rigidly Exact in Recall* (Rigidity).
Corollary: In forming a habit, suffer no violation.

The ability to recall a specific event is a habit. Therefore, in practicing recall, all the laws of habit formation should be obeyed. Easy-going and slovenly recall is doubly wasteful. This applies particularly to the preceding rule and places additional emphasis upon the first impression.

4. *Keep out the Irrelevant* (Relevance).

Corollary: Concentrate on the recall.

If all the memory rules should be reduced to one that rule might be expressed in the single word, "Concentrate." The ability to concentrate attention upon the act in hand is a criterion of a well-developed mind. Suppose that you are preparing for an examination in history. You are rehearsing (not reading over again except to verify) the principal groups of facts to be remembered; each and every individual fact has a rich fringe of associations reaching out into all sorts of matters which have nothing to do with the facts of history, and each of these offers avenues for distraction. Our rule, humiliatingly simple, says: Do not let your mind wander from the matter in hand—these related historical facts. What a waste of human effort results from the violation of this stern rule through lax habits and inherent laziness.

5. *Rest Economically* (Rest).

Corollary: Respect the attention-wave.

It is a familiar fact that we can recall best when the mind is fresh after rest. It is good economy to take a period of rest before a pending serious tax of the memory. But this rule has more important applications. Experiments have shown that we work best mentally when we work periodically rather than in continuous strain. Consciousness has a natural periodicity; the more we favor this periodicity, the more effective we become. The periodicity may be traced in second-waves through two to ten seconds, minute-waves consisting of groups of second-waves, and hour-waves such as the well-known periodicity of the day. Now in recall—and most of our memorizing, as seen above, should be more or less in the nature of recall—we should reach back intensively for a short time and then relax completely for a periodic rest. This periodic activity in simple waves may then be grouped in larger waves. It is a notable fact that those who seem to work the hardest enjoy the most complete relaxation.

We have now approached the pyramid from a third side, Recall, and see in relief the five steps:

Rest: Rest economically

Relevance: Keep out the irrelevant

Rigidity: Be rigidly exact in recall

Repetition: Repeat the recall often

Persistence: Be persistent in the effort to recall

6. *Practice.*

Once more, that which counts in the improvement of recall is systematic practice in recall. So we mount again upon the hard and solid capstone, Practice.

IV. RULES OF RECOGNITION

1. *Recognize the Memory Image as You Would a Friend* (Recognition).

Corollary: "Cut" your friend and he will cut you.

Our thoughts are the children of our minds: our memories are a part of our past. Memory is never complete until the feeling is present that this event has occurred before. It must be recognized as a part of the past but with reference to the present personal associations. This recognition is seldom complete. It is usually based upon a feeling of familiarity and power, and takes the form of a simple belief.

The mere recall is usually automatic and results in action without the intervention of consciousness. Most of my daily activities are in a sense acts of recall, not recognized. To complete the conscious memory this memory image must be singled out and recognized with warmth, as a friend is singled out from a passing throng, and greeted. Apply the principle of recognition in friendship to the recognition of memories and they will be yours. Our children and co-laborers may be about us, but we do not stop to greet them, for they are with us continuously. Many of our most indispensable memories are always with us without intruding upon our time or attention. The rule should be: when memory images come which you desire to fix, greet them warmly and confidingly and they will return to you in time of need.

2. *Cultivate Realistic Imagery in Recognition* (Imagery).

Corollary: Reinstate the original setting.

In meeting a person you shake hands with him, look him in the eye, speak a word, and seal the bond of friendship. So in recalling a friend do not merely entertain an imageless idea of him, but see him, feel him, hear him, feel yourself responding to him, let him stand forth in a natural setting of an earlier meeting and thus make the recognition realistic and tangible. Such experience takes the form of rich and vivid imagery and may be cultivated with success, even if this does not come spontaneously. Its effect is to make the recall intense and rich in detail. You will soon form the habit of having this reinstatement of an earlier meeting a specific one; it may be the first, the last, the most typical, or the most impressive. A memory is not complete until we can localize it in time and place, either directly or indirectly. This habit of concrete imagery has the advantage of resetting the event in the proper time and place, as though we were living the event over again in the original. As toward friends, so toward memories, our feelings of worth, recognition, and attachment reach out to them and bind them to us.

3. *Express the Recognition in Appropriate Action* (Expression).

Corollary: Grow through self-expression.

If you desire to remember the name of a friend be sure that you speak it with full comprehension the moment you reach out your hand upon introduction. Then, when you recall him, recall him by name; and when you meet him again, do not merely say "Good morning," but speak his name as you did upon first meeting and in the recall. More than that, introduce your old friends to new friends from time to time. The application of this principle of friendship to the events and things of daily life is close. The operation is the same as in business; a rule of economy becomes yours only if, in addition to learning it, you apply it to your business relations.

SERVICEABLE MEMORY

4. *Transfer from Conscious to Organic Memory* (Transference).

Corollary: "From conscious effort to ready skill."

At first the memory of each step and each element should be focal in the consciousness of memory and imagination; but, as soon as the skill has been acquired, consciousness is free for other and for higher achievements. Organic memory retains and reproduces its facts so that they result in appropriate expression without the intervention of consciousness, and is therefore easy and reliable. The ability to transfer conscious memories progressively to organic memories is a requisite for great skill, not only in physical dexterity, but in all the higher forms of well-adapted mental achievement.

5. *Learn to Forget the Useless* (Forgetting).

Corollary: Keep your card-catalogue system alive.

Dead timber and the useless accumulate constantly. When an item in your card catalogue has completely outlived its usefulness you remove it. The business of life has its temporary transactions, whose records it would be wasteful to thumb every day after the transactions are closed. The efficient man is the man who lives in the present. It takes deliberate will-power to let the "dead past bury its dead." As our first rule of memory was "Dare to be ignorant," so our last may well be, with all the emphasis we can lay upon it, "Learn to forget."

And this completes our round of the pyramid and we see before us the last ascending scale—the fourth side, Recognition:

Forgetting: Learn to forget the useless
Transference: Transfer to organic memory
Expression: Express recognition in action
Reinstatement: Reinstate the original setting
Recognition: Recognize the memory image

6. *Practice*.

The power of a warm, rich, and serviceable conscious memory is nature's generous gift to all normal men. Practice does not create anything; it merely uses and strengthens. All that has been said of practice should be accepted in this sense: use, enjoy, and it will become and remain your possession. The warning of psychology is: Waste not. So from every side of our pyramid we reach the one all-binding capstone, Practice.

To summarize as an aid in recall let us name the rules in the order given.

SERVICEABLE MEMORY

Impression
  Selection
  Intention
  Attention
  Simplification
  Primacy
  Practice.
Association
  Relationships
  Analysis
  Forcing
  Large Units
  Synthesis
  Practice

Recall
  Persistence
  Repetition
  Rigidity
  Relevance
  Rest
  Practice
Recognition
  Recognition
  Reinstatement
  Expression
  Transference
  Forgetting
  Practice

The reader who has hung the above rules upon the catchword pegs or horns may now review in realistic imagery the legends on the four faces of the pyramid-pedestal, and see the whole crowned with the heroic figure of SERVICEABLE MEMORY.

As the steps of the pyramid are merely parts of the same solid structure, so impression, association, recall, and recognition are merely aspects of the one complex process of memory; the principles here outlined are more far-reaching and interrelated than the statement would suggest.

Who yearns to mount the pyramid? Everybody. Who will mount it? Very, very few. And this is natural and perhaps right. Most of us have decided, mainly through acts of negligence, that the systematic improvement of memory is not worth what it costs. But that does not alter the psychological fact that memory can be improved, nor does it alter the responsibility for its improvement.

Let us not blame our parents for the inheritance of a weak memory. All normal persons have sufficient capacity if only they will use it. To be concrete, the average man does not use above ten per cent. of his actual inherited capacity for memory. He wastes the ninety per cent. by violating natural laws of remembering. Memory is very responsive to training; it is a fit object for conservation. But what most of us attain or conserve is what nature in her beneficent provision preserves for us despite our gross negligence and squandering extravagance.

CHAPTER III

MENTAL EFFICIENCY

Fatigue is one of the commonest signs of inefficiency. Tired mother, tired father, tired teacher, tired preacher, tired clerk, tired president, tired servant, tired master—tired not only in the evening, but often all day; tired, not from excessive work, but usually from wrong methods and habits of work; not always a healthy fatigue after a day's normal work, but a chronic weakness, languor, "living at the tips of one's nerves." Too often the home, the school, the workshop, the office, the social gathering, and the government are in the hands of tired people showing all the signs of nervous fatigue and the resulting irritability. With nervous strain comes nervous instability, and from this many sorts of "vicious circles" develop.

Psychology has no panacea to offer for this condition of mankind; but knowledge of some of the laws of mental work and rest may do much to improve the situation. It is one of the characteristics

69

of mental economy that efficiency and ease seem to go together. This was illustrated in the preceding chapter, which was devoted to a single intensive example of mental economy in a specific mental process—memory. (To illustrate this fact further I shall present a few cases in which the recognition of certain mental laws would result in the escape from a part of this fatigue-tendency through habits of work and rest, and at the same time increase both efficiency and ease. These isolated cases are chosen to indicate some of the manifold bearings of psychology upon the conservation of mental energy. The six brief sketches illustrate the following principles respectively: (1) That sense-training is the fundamental step in the conservation of mental effort through education; (2) that education should be based upon the natural growth from within, through the principle of self-expression; (3) that in all mental work systems of serviceable automatisms should be established progressively; (4) that the principle of specialization should be applied both in vocations and in avocations; (5) that rest or vacations should be based on daily rather than yearly periods; and (6) that a midday nap is a good investment.)

MENTAL EFFICIENCY

THE ATTENTION-WAVE: SENSE TRAINING VERSUS INFORMATION

In measuring the keenness of the perception of weight in thirty girls in a normal training class in gymnastics I found one girl who was nearly three times as keen as the average girl in the class. The test determined how small difference in weight each observer could detect by lifting in rapid succession two small boxes which differed slightly in weight. The keener the sense of weight, the smaller the appreciated difference. The test was very simple; merely to lift the two boxes as carefully as possible and say which appeared to be the heavier. Twenty-nine girls proceeded in a haphazard way and lifted the boxes several times, trying to get an average judgment; the exceptional girl paused to think what she was to do before lifting, then lifted each box once and immediately gave her judgment. Observe, she was prepared to trust her first impression; she knew what to do; and she concentrated all her energies upon that specific task at the right moment.

This is typical of all sense observation. Twenty-nine out of thirty are wasteful and dull in their sense-perceptions because they do not concentrate. The one who proceeds economically stands out as an object of remark. The question arises, Why could not the ratio be reversed by right training, so that the twenty-nine would show the high efficiency, and but one remain deficient, possibly by reason of defective mentality?

The illustration is still more striking when it is noted that the twenty-nine were more or less flurried, dissatisfied, and wearied by their performance, while the one of marked achievement worked with apparent ease and comfort; indeed, she seemed to rest except at the very moments of actual lifting.

This difference in personal ability may be in-

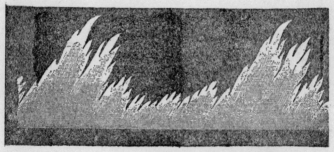

Fig. 1

terpreted in terms of the attention-wave. Consciousness is never a placid stream; it moves more or less boldly in waves like the breakers on the ocean beach. There are large waves, and within these are wavelets and ripples of various degrees, as is represented schematically in Fig. 1. This change in the form and degree of consciousness we ordinarily speak of in terms of attention; hence the expression, attention-waves.

Figuratively, we may say that there is a given quantity of the mental stream available for any given activity, *e. g.,* for perception. This amount may be made available in different forms. The effectiveness of the stream depends upon the distribution of the energy, *i. e.,* upon the form of the stream.

The contour of the stream of consciousness for a given time, say three seconds, may be represented by three typical attention-wave forms, as in Fig. 2.

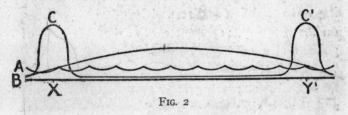

FIG. 2

If the three areas described by the curves A, B, and CC' above the base line were equal, this would denote the fact that there is merely a difference in distribution of a given quantity of the stream. It is also assumed that the effectiveness of consciousness is represented by the height to which the wave rises at the critical moments of action, in this case X and

Y. A then represents an inferior form of consciousness flowing in a stream of small wavelets and not rising far above the dead level. B represents a better form of consciousness in that the wave rises to a higher level; but the maximum point does not occur at a favorable time, the crest coming between the two critical moments, X and Y. CC' represents an ideal form for this particular case, as each of the two crests, C and C', reaches its maximum at a critical moment.

In this figure it is seen that CC' has two crests representing work at the effective moments and that between these there is a wide trough representing full relaxation and rest. The other two curves, on the contrary, represent continual strain, lack of poise, and a semi-aimless and unfruitful lag.

On the above assumption the efficiency of the form CC' is as much greater than that of forms A and B as it rises higher than these at the moments of action; and it is as much more restful than these as it falls below them during the non-critical period.

In other words, the efficient is the restful and easy. The one keen observer in the perception of weight was of the CC' type. The other girls scattered their energies as in curves A and B and thus lessened the value of their sensibilities.

The lesson from this illustration may be expressed by analogy. If you want to lift a hundred-pound sack of flour into a bin do not tug away at it with a continuous strain of from twenty-five to seventy-five pounds, only to see the sack unmoved; but lift the hundred pounds instantly and then, after successful achievement, rest completely. The analogy is true; if you wish to test how heavy an object is, do not make a non-intensive, prolonged, and therefore fruitless effort; but make the observation intensively adapted and, therefore, with largest promise of success.

This basic principle of concentration of attention lies at the very foundation of our every-day work. Sense perception often takes the form of a continuous strain, relatively ineffective, because we do not realize that it may be reduced to specific moments of intensive activity separated by comparatively long periods of restful relaxation. Psychology teaches that, by forming right habits of attention, we may improve at the same time in efficiency and ease, and thereby vastly increase our comfort as we increase the value of our lives.

Dawdling is the common violation of this principle of efficiency. Schools often encourage it. It is the aimless and ineffective strain and dull endeavor that prevents attention from rising to heights of efficiency. To the child, and even to the average teacher, sense experience is a kaleidoscopic medley, and the effort at training seems futile.

The first psychological step which can direct training in sense efficiency is a recognition of the elements involved. The fundamental factor is the adjustment of attention, which means using the available mental energy in the right form and at the right time. In sense perception this may be reduced to two factors; first, attention to the impression by itself, and, second, attention to the comparison of impressions. The former gives us keen sensitiveness and the latter keen discrimination. Discrimination is the ability to detect difference and represents the capacity for the intellectual use of a sense. Each of us has a measurable sensitiveness to brightness, color, space, and time of visual sensations, and likewise for corresponding attributes of sound, odor, taste, pressure, temperature, and pain; and, for each of these various sense attributes we have also a measurable keenness in discrimination.

This recognition of two elemental capacities common to all the senses offers a starting point for the pedagogy of sense training. Training in any of the senses should have this twofold aim—sensitiveness and discrimination.

Children should be taught early the habit of trusting their senses, and particularly the first impression. This training should be rigid, systematic, and unremitting—a goal in itself. No amount of information stored up in the early years can be a substitute for the mastery of the senses.

Sense perception is the basis of the intellectual life. With the habit of keen sense perception for color goes the keen memory for color; the creative imagination is likely to be powerful in proportion to the fidelity and vividness of the image of past experience. The same principle extends even to reasoning; for this preëminently is characterized by the power of concentration upon the ideas and images of past experience.

In modern psychology we have adopted the motto: "Not psychology, but to psychologize." So in all, and particularly in early, instruction our aim should be, not the amassing of information, but the training of the powers of the mind.

As between the receiving of information and the development of the sensory organism, educational principles emphasize the latter, but the prevailing practice is based upon the former alternative. It is so easy: those who do not know how to teach are often naturally adept in imparting information. It is so satisfying: the lecturer, from the kindergarten teacher to the university professor, can cast the statement of fact in such lucid and artistic form that he is set all aglow with self-appreciation. The pupils approve: the ready-made goods seem attractive, and there is comfort in the freedom from effort.

The efficient training of the sensory organism, on the other hand, is very difficult. As yet educational psychology has affected practice in sense training very little. Theoretically, educational psychology has furnished an approach to the pedagogy of sense training by giving an insight into the nature and function of sensory experience, showing that it involves only two elementary factors, namely, sensitiveness and discrimination; that these are present in all the senses; that, aside from normality in the structure of the sense organ, the determining factor of sensitiveness and discrimination is central, a common factor for all the senses; that by right habits of attention efficient keenness of all the senses may be developed far above the prevailing average; that these habits once established continue and form an inestimable asset of power; that, as a result of high efficiency in sensory acquisition, the information which is vital to life will be gained incidentally; that keen perception, the foundation of intelligence, is a condition for true and vital imagination, faithful memory, clear perception, in-

cisive reasoning, and efficient action. Our ideal is
not individuals stocked with information, but individuals fitted with trained capacities; knowledge
is not always power, but a well-disciplined mind is
power. The key to the training of the senses is the
habit of directing attention in efficient, economic,
and restful waves.

GROWTH THROUGH SELF-EXPRESSION

Instruction does not always aid. As a child I
had the advantage of learning arithmetic under a
teacher who did not know the subject. She had
difficulty with "fractions," but had the good grace
to leave us to our own devices. We discovered that
after reading the introductory statement for each
new section and performing the required operations
with confidence in our own efforts, we had but little
need of the teacher. This gave us a delightful
feeling of power and incentive. We found no insuperable difficulty at any point; we mastered the
subject from day to day, and trusted ourselves.
The impetus thus gained was a permanent asset.
Although I later had good teachers, I proceeded by
the same method with algebra, geometry, trigo-
nometry, and conic sections, and, for the pleasure

of it, usually kept in advance of the class assignments.

As arithmetic is ordinarily taught, the teacher gives the explanation and the pupil looks on; the teacher gets the training and the pupil is so handicapped that, for each successive stage, he needs the teacher more and more, and gradually becomes dependent and deprived of the rightful help of his own resources.

What is true of arithmetic in this respect is true of the teaching of every other subject. "Education through self-expression" should be a motto of the school, the home, and the church, as well as of the playground. The prevailing practice is very different. What the teacher explains is already known by one-third of the members of the class; it is "above the heads," or not noticed, by another third of the class; and on a generous assumption it may be profitable information or experience to the remaining one-third of the class. Not only is there a loss of time for two-thirds of the class, but sensibility is blunted and bad habits of attention are formed.

The error lies in the neglect of the principle of self-expression and, as a result, the enforcing of a lock-step system of thinking and acting. The solution lies in the organization of instruction on the order of social competition with an elastic system of promotion based on achievement.)

A good illustration of the application of this method of elementary instruction is found in the "Business College." The pupil may enter at any time of the year with almost any kind of preparation. There are certain things that he must learn. He soon starts in actual business, keeping his books, making actual transactions with his bank, and associating with embryo merchants. He is encouraged to do as much business in a day as he can. No one stands in his way. He is thrown upon his own resources; if he makes a mistake in addition he must discover it himself and suffer the consequences. If he starts out to borrow or to ask for help he soon learns the error of his way; and, best of all, his success in this make-believe business depends upon his ability to deal successfully with his comrades in current coin and good will.

The method possesses merit. The student is not confined to a lock-step system; he begins where he needs to begin, and goes as fast as he can, and no faster; no time is wasted in receiving explanations of things that he already knows or in listening to discussions that he cannot comprehend. He is thrown into actual social intercourse with his associates; his success depends not alone upon the development of his knowledge, but also upon his ability to get along with men, which is no small part of education. The application of these principles to elementary and secondary instruction has long been recognized as an ideal; but it takes generations to put it into operation. Our educational system and its setting must be made over in many respects; equipment, teachers, text-books, and even the ideals of the authorities must be radically changed; and, until these advances gradually are attained together, no such enterprise can be entirely successful. But it is feasible, and need not involve any increase in the teaching force or equipment. The principal expense will be demanded for the command of genius for organization.

The principles of this method are these: set the child to work as nearly as possible at his highest level; introduce a system of social competition; let him be free to move, to ask questions, and to co-operate with others; introduce a system of coöperative examination and tests; advance him as soon as he masters his tasks, and no sooner; in short, whenever possible, let him do, instead of having things done for him; and make the habit of initiative a condition of his survival in the school-world.

On these principles it would be possible to re-form any grade of the public schools by introducing an individual or coöperative group method of instruction in all the subjects, as is commonly practiced in laboratories. The injunction of educational psychology might well read: Teach less, and give the child more opportunity to learn.

The psychological justification of this principle of self-expression lies in the fact that it stands for development according to natural law; it insists that we shall undertake only that for which we are prepared, that we shall acquire that which our organization—mental and physical—needs, that mastery gained shall be fixed by use, and that the only true growth is from within.

The great achievement of modern child-study is the discovery of the individual. The sequel to child-study will be child adjustment; and, in this, the demand in the interest of economic and efficient growth is the opportunity for self-expression, the privilege of the child to live at his own personal, highest level.

MASTERY THROUGH TRANSFER TO LOWER MENTAL LEVELS

There are various levels of mental work, from the highest, which is represented by the most intensely concentrated consciousness, down to the lowest mentality which borders on the purely physiological. In proportion to the height of the level the mental process involves an extensive outlay of energy, and is unstable, modifiable, and capable of new adjustments. Conversely, in proportion to the lowness of the level, the mental process involves

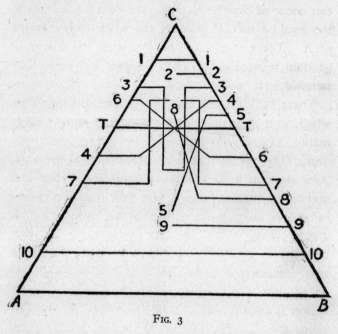

FIG. 3

economic expenditure of energy, and is constant, reliable, and efficient for routine work.

Let us represent a cross section of the stream of mental processes at a given moment by a triangle,

ABC, Fig. 3. The apex of this triangle then represents the highest, and the base the lowest mental level. The tapering from the base to the apex indicates that the higher the given level, the smaller must be the relative amount of mental activity that can occur at that level. In other words, the lower the level of mental process, the more there can be of it. There is not an abrupt break, but rather a gradual transition from the highest and rarely attainable level to the lowest.

There is, however, one convenient dividing line which is a permanent and definable distinguishing mark. That is known as the threshold of consciousness. The mental processes which are above that level are said to be conscious, and those below are said to be subconscious. The presence or absence of waking awareness of the mental process is the distinguishing mark. In our triangle this division line, TT, is placed relatively high to indicate the fact that conscious processes are relatively few as compared with the subconscious. The vast mass of common mental acts are subconscious. It also denotes the fact that the conscious mentality rests upon a foundation of subconscious mentality.

The lines 1-10 crossing the triangle represent typical courses that mental acts may take with respect to mental level. Though the figure is crude and fragmentary, it suggests certain facts about the flux from level to level. The stream of mental processes is always in one direction—impression, elaboration, expression. Any of these stages may be high or low as compared with the other; 4, *e. g.,* represents a subconscious impression which rises in the elaboration and results in a distinctly conscious expression; 6 represents the reverse; 7 typifies the act which originates in subliminal impression, rises to clear consciousness in the elaboration, only to drop and be expressed automatically. The general fact here observed is that in sinking to a lower mental level a mental act settles irregularly in its various parts. In the process of becoming automatic it goes through a complex state of flux in its parts and gradually settles down as a unified automatism at a low level. Some part of the act first attempted is done with full consciousness throughout. In a series of irregular and complex oscillations up and down in continued repetition this element gradually sinks from consciousness and new elements in the situation become focal. Thus element after element in an act is formed, fitted, and set into a larger, stable whole—a serviceable automatism.

In this scheme level 1 represents mental activity of the most highly plastic order, conscious throughout—variable, expensive, awkward, and difficult; while level 10 represents the most stable order, subconscious throughout—old, fixed, economic, graceful, and easy. The intervening levels represent the more or less characteristic gradations between these extremes by which an act of the first type may gradually be reduced to the tenth type through practice. The whole represents very crudely the tendency of the course normally taken in the acquisition of skill.

The striking of a chord on the piano involves more or less simultaneously the operation of scores, not to say hundreds, of processes, each of which has itself been a specific object of consciousness at some stage in the training. Among such elements of the act of playing are the factors involved in the reading and interpretation of the score, in the personal reaction to the musical idea it represents, and in the form, force, order, and rate of movement in the expression. In effective playing this series of processes must flow more or less automatically; the player must not interrupt them by conscious effort, and he must be free from consciousness of them in order that his mind may occupy itself with the feelings and ideas to be expressed, and to judge the result progressively as an expression of musical effect and not as the result of a conscious coördination between musical ideas and finger-movements in playing.

As the pianist profits throughout his life by having acquired, for example, a particular form of finger movement or touch, so in all our effective work we depend upon the gradual accumulation of those processes which can be done better automatically at the lower mental levels.

In whatever mental achievement we desire proficiency our goal should be to master the elementary factors involved, one at a time, so that they may be transferred to the lowest level. This having been accomplished, the higher consciousness may be free to be engrossed in vital acquisition and in the more general processes of feeling, thought, and personal choice.

The efficient man is the man who, in all that he undertakes, selects those achievements which are worth while and then masters their elements. That is, instead of being satisfied to do all things in a wasteful, variable, expensive, awkward, and difficult way, he gradually reduces those that are worth while to the familiar, fixed, graceful, and easy procedure. He applies to all his achievements the principle which the expert applies in the acquisition of great skill. It is the application of this principle to the "little things of life" that counts most.

SPECIALIZATION A MEANS OF CONSERVATION

It has been set forth that mental energy is best conserved by cultivating automatisms and adhering to them. The movements of a skilled pianist, the writing of an expert stenographer, typewriting with the "touch" system at high speed, the expert accountant footing up long columns of figures at a rapid glance, the artist creating a complex object of meaning and beauty with a few rapid strokes of the brush, seem remarkable achievements yet performed with ease, grace, and accuracy. They are the result of specialization. Specialization has been the key to advancement in the various arts; and it is possible for all normal persons to acquire in any daily occupation, physical or mental, the same sort of skill that the pianist, the stenographer, the accountant, and the artist display.

Nothing is done well until it is reduced to an automatic stage. We are apt to dissipate our mental power by not doing anything in particular. It may be safely said that in many mental activities we exert a wasteful effort. The introduction of "scientific management" in manufacture and industry proceeds by simplifying processes and increasing efficiency through specialization.

The same method applied to daily life would advise thus: "Select a specific occupation that you like; master it until you have five, or ten, or fifty-fold the efficiency that an untrained worker may have; stay by this occupation and do not dabble in any other; be ready for advancement in your field of work, for, no matter how small or commonplace the work may be, there is abundant opportunity for fresh achievement; work intensively and only for short hours. Then, be it brick-laying, teaching, or painting, you will accomplish more than your share, you will conserve your energies, and you will have abundant time for an avocation, recreation, leisure, and rest." And the same principle must be applied to the pursuit of avocations, social accomplishments, recreations, and even rest. "A little of everything and much of something" should be the rule.

To be an expert in one thing carries with it power over other situations. An accomplished singer may be unable to do anything but sing; yet his art gives him a station, a social ranking which his ability enables him to maintain. The possession of high skill or efficiency in one field gives one confidence in self and often spreads to other activities in such a way that a man may live at the level of his highest achievement, however specialized this may be;

whereas a person without specialized automatisms must live at the level of the untrained.

A single far-fetched illustration will suffice. In this country many girls go directly into high-school teaching upon graduation from college; and this is a common story; too severe nervous strain—deteriorating health and beauty—rest to recuperate—a neurotic wife and mother. This picture may be extreme, but it is a fact that a large portion of the young women who do not intend to make teaching a profession for life, but teach for five consecutive years in the high school, acquire some marked tendencies to nervous breakdown. If only ten per cent of them suffered in this respect the sacrifice would be too great, but the percentage is much higher. Teaching is now a profession, and ordinarily it is not good mental economy to follow this profession temporarily while the mind is bent on something else. But assuming that the young woman is going to take this extravagant course, wasting precious life-energies in establishing herself in a skilled occupation which she does not intend to pursue permanently (and she can show many reasons for so doing), the condition might be met by allowing her to undertake about two-thirds of the usual service for the first year, three-fourths for the second, four-fifths for the third, and assume full work in the fourth year, with corresponding advances in salary. By such a system the progressive adaptation would prepare for a gradual increase in application and lessen the strain involved.

VACATIONS LONG OR SHORT

Twenty-five years ago vacations were not prominent. At present men and women in all callings, from the highest to the lowest, measure the flow of life by the regular recurrence of vacations. Pulpit, schoolroom, factory, kitchen, and farm must provide "days off." This tendency is in harmony with the development of scientific management in human efficiency. But it may well be asked whether we have not gone vacation-mad.

The vacation has two purposes: first, rest from regular occupation; and, second, diversion for enrichment of life.

Psychology makes a plea for both of these, and it also urges that they be set off in a clear-cut way from the work of the daily calling. "Work while you work and play while you play." But psychology sounds a warning against the present tendency to make the periods too long and too far apart. The natural period of work and rest is not the year but the twenty-four hour day.

It is wrong for the university professor, the preacher, the merchant, and the woman in society to work desperately and allow the physiological machinery to run down for ten months because there will be two months in which to recuperate. Yet that is the American vacation, and in most cases it is unwise. This storm and stress method of adjustment in work and recreation is a characteristic of the adolescence of our nation. Another half-century may witness a better adaptation. This better adaptation will consist in a more economical distribution of our periods of rest and recreation in accordance with the principles of the so-called work-curve, which is a psychological standard of the most favorable periods for work and rest, or change of occupation. Such a norm is being established gradually for many kinds of work and rest. The curve of the attention-wave is an illustration of a work-curve on a small scale.

Vacation trips are needed and take much time, but they are often of the nature of work rather than rest. A period of exceptional quiet for several days once a year is highly desirable. But to keep the mind and body in healthful condition all the year around requires rest and recreation distributed through the year.

There is a tendency for all kinds of work to become more intensive. But just as efficiency increases with increasing intensiveness, so the organism demands corresponding relaxation. The day seems to be the most normal period for systematic relaxation. The night's sleep is nature's provision for this purpose; but as our work grows more intensive this natural rhythm needs to be supplemented by stated periods of rest, fresh air, and relaxation during the day.

To take a specific case, a teacher will be vastly better off if he gets systematic out-of-door exercise, with a sense of freedom, at least three to seven times a week, and works the year around, than if he shuts himself up in a school-room or study for nine months and then trusts to a three-months' vacation for recuperation.

The reason this warning needs to be sounded is that the tendency at the present time is to avoid vacations until the organism sounds alarm; and that is a very dangerous and uneconomic procedure. The systematic distribution of short periods of rest and recreation throughout the week will make it possible to keep the system constantly in good condition and good running order instead of having it seriously run down through long stress and strain only to be built up slowly in a wasteful way.

THE MIDDAY NAP

A personal incident may be pardoned. While at Yale University I approached the physical director, Dr. Seaver, on a balmy April day and asked him to prescribe a tonic. He looked me in the eye, and the following conversation ensued: "What is the first thing you do after dinner?" "I go to work—study." "Are you a gentleman?" "I am trying to be." "Are you a Christian?" "I am trying to be." "A Christian gentleman, and take no rest after dinner!"

I took that rest tonic as prescribed, have continued to take it, and have had no need of any other. It has assumed the form of a fifteen-minute midday nap, my principal meal coming at noon. Realizing the great benefit in this, I have been interested in casting about for a psychological justification thereof. This I find chiefly in the curve of sleep. The curve of sleep, as measured by the relative stimulus required for awakening a sleeper at different stages of the sleep, is shown in Fig. 4 (Kohlschütter). The numbers at the bottom indicate hours of sleep; the height of the curve shows the height, in centimeters, from which a ball must be dropped upon a metal plate in order to awaken the sleeping person. The curve shows that the normal sleeper falls immediately into a profound sleep which reaches the maximum at the end of the first hour, then becomes lighter very rapidly during the second hour, and remains light for the rest of the night. Cumulatively, the sleeper

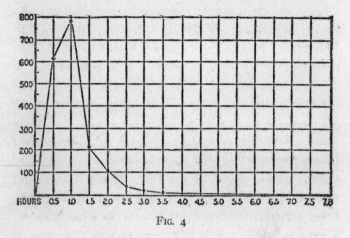

FIG. 4

gets more needed rest out of the first one-fourth of the night than out of the remaining three-fourths.

This general form of the sleep-curve has been verified for various conditions. The feature which concerns us is that the greatest benefit from normal sleep, night or day, comes from the very first part of it. From this we may derive a principle of mental economy: (Cut short the long light sleep of the late morning hours and substitute a short sleep at some favorable time during the work day. Fifteen minutes of sleep after the heaviest work and the main meal of the day will count more for efficiency than five times fifteen minutes of sleep in the morning. The curve of day sleep has the same form as the curve of night sleep; but its duration as thus measured is usually far less. From ten to twenty minutes would cover the period of deepest sleep in the day-rest of a normal brainworker.

But several conditions enter into the problem. Many persons cannot fall into sound sleep in such a short time during the day. The ability to go to sleep, however, is largely a matter of habit, which most persons may readily acquire by reasonable persistence and favorable conditions. The nap must be so taken that it shall not interfere with the night's rest. The most favorable duration of the nap varies with different individuals, but it should not be long under any circumstances. It must be so taken that it shall not result in stupor at awakening. Taking the nap in a cushioned easy-chair, with the body slightly reclining, will prevent the rush of blood to the brain. But the position of the body must be such as to secure free and deep breathing.

The advantage of sleep is that it gives the most adequate relaxation of the body and mind. An after-dinner cigar furnishes relaxation and repose; but the feeling of restfulness after a quiet smoke is due in part to the artificial soothing, while the restfulness felt after a nap is the natural feeling of restoration.

CHAPTER IV

MENTAL HEALTH

What am I? The simplest thinker asks this question in his musings about life, and the savant pursues it more and more intensively. It is the fundamental question of psychology. The whole science of psychology is largely a specialized answer to this question.

AN INVENTORY OF SELF

To obtain a point of view for the discussion, and to secure a judgment at first hand, the reader is asked to take an inventory of himself. It is important that he shall make this inventory in person and not merely accept it. Let it be an exercise in self-observation or introspection with note-book in hand. Lay aside the reading and consider the question more personally, "What am I? In what respects may I consider my nature?"

In rough outlines the self-examination has probably taken some such course as the following: I am a bodily being. My body is a carefully constructed system of systems. There are head, trunk, limbs, internal organs, and sense organs. There are transportation apparatus, heating apparatus, ventilation apparatus, communication apparatus, a chemical laboratory, and a governing organization, all highly perfected systems working within me. For this body I must eat, sleep, breathe, and exercise. The first that I knew of myself was my body. I can see it and feel it. I am sure that I am a bodily being.

I am an intellectual being. I am a mind capable of knowing. As an intellectual being I can see, hear, taste, smell, imagine, remember, form ideas, make judgments, reason to conclusions, be guided by rational feelings, and act intelligently. I can do these things as surely as I can eat and run with my body. Indeed, I contrast myself with the idiot and the insane and rejoice in the fact that I am a rational being. My work is intellectual, my avocations are intellectual, my aspirations are intellectual. Even in my physical labor it is the intellect that guides and governs my movements. I am in large part what I know.

I am a social being. I am a member of a family which I love. I am a member of a social group by coöperation in occupation. I am a free and active citizen of a commonwealth and a nation. What makes life worth living? Friends!—things to do for friends, the appreciation of friends, the awards of friendship, and social achievements. I am dependent upon social coöperation for protection, sustenance, happiness, and development. I cannot think of myself as not caring for anybody, not helping anybody, not being helped by anybody. My capacities and my purposes are social, and the essence of my social life is mental. I am love, fear, hatred, aspiration, generosity, truth, sympathy, malevolence, benevolence—a medley of social feelings, attitudes, and acts. Truly, I am a social being.

I am a moral being. I have many ideas of what is right and what is wrong. I demand justice, equity, kindness, truth, and safety. I hate injustice, unfairness, meanness, and falsehood. I take pleasure in doing right and feel remorse after having done wrong. I fear temptation and struggle continually toward a fairly high goal of life. My friends are my friends because they can trust me. My business intercourse rests upon the assumption of moral integrity. True, I am not able to reach such ethical standards as I entertain. My whole life is a moral struggle. My loves, interests, achievements, friendships, and influence are moral affairs. My will is the supreme living power within me. For good or for evil, I am a moral being.

I am an æsthetic being. My joy of living comes from a sense of beauty. I derive pleasure from flowers, fields, air, water, mountains, and skies, as though they had their existence for my pleasure. I am moved by the beauty of a human figure, face, smile, or tear; by human tact and taste, even by outward dress and manners. The ugly in nature and art repels me. Music kindles my emotions; pictures not only give me information, but they inspire me with a joy of living. My home, my dress, my garden would be cold and barren were it not for their appeal to my sense of beauty. Bodily, intellectual, social, and moral life get their greatest sweetness and give their fullest sense of luxury when they are beautiful. It is my great regret that I cannot do more to create the beautiful for myself and for others, for one of my loftiest cravings and a constant leverage for my higher life is my sense of beauty.

I am a religious being. True, I realize my great shortcomings, but this very realization of the sense of obligation and a craving for a higher life is proof of my religious nature. I feel religious impulses welling up instinctively. I have a sort of practical creed in the process of development as I live it. I am a religious being.

The items here enumerated in the make-up of the self have probably been verified by the reader, for, although they take various forms, it is a commonplace fact that we are bodily beings, intellectual beings, social beings, moral beings, æsthetic beings, and religious beings.

THE NATURE OF MENTAL HEALTH

The object of this inventory has been to show that we are essentially mental beings, and that mental health, therefore, is not a side issue to physical health, for all these selves which we have listed, except the first, are essentially mental selves. Their nature is psycho-physical.

With this inventory in mind let us now broach the question, "What is mental health?" The answer may be stated in terms of our inventory: mental health has reference to health of intellect, health of social feelings and attitudes, health of conscience, health of sensitiveness to beauty and goodness, and health of feelings of dependence and responsiveness to a Being greater than ourselves.

Health of the intellectual self, for example, means healthy sensations, imaginations, memories, ideas, judgments, impulses, attention, and voluntary action. All these are extremely susceptible to disorders. There are all sorts of gradations of disorders, from the common forms of slightly depraved sensory tendencies, through lurid imagination, heart breaking memories and delusions, and loss of self control, even to the extreme deprivations as in imbecility, idiocy, and insanity. Health of the social self means health of the social feelings, attitudes, and responses, such as tend to maintain a social organism. It is the social virtues as against the social vices. Vice and crime are social sickness. Health of the moral self means a sound and effective conscience. Remorse is moral suffering, the penalty of moral wrong. Moral perversion and obtuseness are the expression of a retarded and diseased conscience. Health of the æsthetic self means a well-developed capacity for observing, appreciating, and experiencing beauty. The person who cannot find beauty in a blade of grass, in a starlit heaven, or in a deed of human kindness is ethically in bad health, if not æsthetically withered and dead. Health of the religious self means rational and responsive feelings toward God, which result in progressive realization of a life of truth, goodness, and beauty.

For the purpose of a practical appreciation and

conception of mental health it is necessary to bear in mind three facts: First, we become what we are, mentally and physically, through growth—development. Just as our arms grow strong through exercise, so our intellectual capacities, our conscience, and our sentiments are realized only through exercise. Mental health is, therefore, not merely a preservation of what we have, but is rather a full, progressive, and continuous development of our inherited capacities. Health is not negative, the avoidance of acts that may injure our minds, but most essentially positive—the doing of that which shall give our minds a better and fuller growth. Second, health is a matter of degree. No one is in perfect health, physically or mentally. It is not idiocy, insanity, or death that we are trying to ward off; it is the thousands of daily little ills which singly seem insignificant but which in the cumulative effect are disastrous. Third, we are accustomed to our small imperfections and failings and are therefore in danger of not realizing how every little step in our lives counts for weal or for woe. Their very frequency leads us to regard them as natural in the course of events. Many of us do not realize the woe until it comes with a shock, often too late.

THE RELATION OF MENTAL HEALTH TO PHYSICAL HEALTH

Mental health depends upon bodily health. The dependence of mind upon body may be observed, for example, in the commonplace act of unwise eating. To eat too much, to eat too frequently, to eat too rapidly, to eat too great a variety; to eat when tired, to eat when thinking hard, to eat improperly prepared food, to eat merely to please the hostess, to eat merely for good fellowship; to eat too many sweets or sours, to eat that which is too cold, too hot, or too rich; to eat to stimulate, to eat to soothe, to eat to save, to eat to tickle the palate, even to eat to eat, tends to becloud the mind just to the extent that it acts unfavorably upon the body. Interference with digestion is absolutely sure to affect our mental health. So with air, exercise, and all other conditions that affect the body. Many a man's view of the world, many a harsh treatment of others may be traceable to dyspepsia, to cold feet, to a tender corn, or to a degenerate biceps.

The reason for this lies in the fact that the brain is the organ of the mind—not that the brain produces the mind, but that mental processes and brain processes are in some way correlated and interdependent—and the health of the brain depends directly or indirectly upon the health of other parts of the body. Interference with any part of the circulation, respiration, or secretion in the body invariably affects the brain, and in so far as it affects the brain it affects mental function. The body is a medium for the mind; if the body is ill the mind will be affected. Hereupon rests the first law of mental health: "Keep the body in good repair."

Bodily health depends upon mental health. The control and care of the body are primarily mental affairs. Our use of the body in eating, working, and playing is governed by our sensations, imaginations, impulses, will, and intelligence. A man builds a house which becomes a means of protection and a source of comfort for him. The house would not have been built or kept in repair except for his interests and his efforts. So the development of the bodily organism has taken place in response to the needs of the mind, and has been shaped largely under its control. A most significant proof of this dependence of the body upon the mind is to be found in the fact that the body cannot develop without use—as in work, or in play—and it is the mind that puts it to use.

Our mental states affect all the physiological processes of the body. Feelings and ideas modify the beat of the heart, the action of the stomach, of the liver, of the intestines, of the secreting glands, and of all other functional systems of the body.

Many diseases of mankind are caused by mental conditions, and many are curable by mental procedure. Mental healing has been practiced in all ages, and is perhaps more prevalent at the present time than ever before. It is used unscrupulously by quacks and charlatans, effectively though often indiscreetly in the interests of religion, judiciously by physicians in connection with the regular administration of drugs, and more or less scientifically by physicians trained in the science and art of mental therapeutics.

If, then, the body is in countless ways so much influenced by the mind, we may lay down this as the first law of physical health: "Keep the mind in good repair."

Epitomizing the argument, we find that mental health means health of the mental selves—the intellectual, the social, the moral, the æsthetic, and the religious selves; not merely the avoidance of ill health, but growth, exercise, and use; not merely the avoidance of fatal disease, but freedom from the little ills which burrow in our minds; not merely the avoidance of breakdown, but pride in the possession of a sound and well-developed mind.

To this end two principles may serve; to secure mental health keep the body in good repair; and to secure bodily health, keep the mind in good repair.

TEN RULES OF WISE LIVING

Such is the nature of mental health. Turning to the normative side, we may consider the principles of mental hygiene that psychology offers. Mental hygiene is as large a field as that of physical hygiene; the two are inseparable. Psychiatry, or mental pathology, is being reorganized in the foundation of scientific psychology. Psychological principles are applied to the treatment of mental defectives. The consulting psychologist is coming to be recognized in education, especially with reference to the education and care of the mentally abnormal child. Religious movements apply psychological principles for the betterment of the human mind. Efforts to secure mental conservation are expressed in preventive medicine for the elimination of causes of mental contagion, mental waste and mental degeneracy, by deliberately planning for the establishment of a favorable mental environment. In short, we are beginning to realize that we are in a very real sense mental beings, and that it is possible and worth while to exercise the same sort of care for our mental welfare as for our physical health.

The keynote of this book is mental health. Each of the preceding chapters has dealt with one or another of its specific aspects. It would be premature to generalize from the scattered scientific data of applied psychology in all its fields. The advice of the family physician consists, not so much in the prescription of medicinal remedies as in the professional stamp of approval and commendation of nature's beneficent forces, such as fresh air, good light, pure water, a wholesome diet, and rest. Similarly applied psychology may accomplish the most general service by turning the light of scientific scrutiny upon certain commonly available though often neglected mental resources that have been justified anew and in a deeper sense through scientific observation and research. As fresh air has been rediscovered for the consumptive, so certain common elements in the environment upon which the mind feeds have been rediscovered as fountains of mental health. Avoiding the more technical statements, I shall bring together some rules and views from the thinkers of the past, and attempt to show that a whole-hearted recognition of these is of first and most lasting importance for an attitude of healthy-mindedness. These rules will be recognized as familiar maxims of wise living.

I. *Know thyself.* We do not know ourselves. We are as a rule ignorant of the physiology and hygiene of our bodies. We do not know the nature, scope, and limitations of our intellectual capacities—their dangers, their charms, their possibilities. It is often by mere chance that we find ourselves in the possession of this or that hitherto unrecognized intellectual endowment. We do not know our social powers. We are continually struggling to determine how we stand—whether we are conceited, whether we are arrogant, whether we are generous, what social capacities we possess and what we lack. We do not know our moral selves. Human relations continually reveal to us depths of goodness and badness within ourselves and in others. We do not know our æsthetic selves. Treasures of beauty on all sides are in great part lost through our ignorance. Seeing, we see not; hearing, we hear not the impressions thrust upon us. The more we learn of these aspects of our nature, the more we discover that we do not know; as we ask one question of nature, nature asks us ten.

PSYCHOLOGY IN DAILY LIFE

After a first course in psychology students often remark that they "live in a different world." The facts of mental nature reveal the conditions and the significance of the wholesomeness of life. An inventory of the mental selves at first hand cannot fail to contribute to the enhancement of mental health, if it be employed seriously from day to day. Knowledge of mind comes late in the development of the individual, and often scarcely at all; in ignorance we all too often blindly trample upon the delicate flowers of mental life, and experience nothing but the prick of the thorns. Mental retardation, distortion, and decay spring in a very real sense from lack of knowledge and from false information about the nature and power of the various selves. The greatest mental deprivation is the non-realization of the higher selves. The great psychological movements in preventive medicine aim to revitalize the ancient doctrine: "Knowledge of self is the first virtue."

II. *Learn self-control.* The noblest of ancient philosophers taught that the reason people do not lead a good life is that they do not know how. Teach them justice and they will be just; tell them what temperance is, and they will be temperate. But he was not entirely correct. We do not do all that we know to be right and good. We agree with Portia that:

"If to do were as easy as to know what were good to do, chapels had been churches, and poor men's cottages princes' palaces. It is a good divine that follows his own instructions: I can easier teach twenty what were good to be done, than be one of twenty to follow mine own teaching."

This principle of self-control has taken three aspects: (1) use the knowledge you have—put it to use—all of it; (2) make your own thought a little superior to circumstances; and (3) identify yourself with the universal law.

The first law of self-control in its bare plainness is this: "Live as well as you know how"—not in the sense of a makeshift, but in the sense of active effort.

"Rally the good in the depths of thyself!" The world is what we make it: biography, the history of culture, the history of philosophy, and the history of religion abound in illustrations of personal attitudes, national movements, philosophical teachings, and religious creeds built upon this precept. Social conditions are too commonly regarded as dispensations of Providence. Few realize to what extent the psycho-physical environment is of our own making.

The second law is the doctrine of Stoicism which teaches a valuable lesson of the supremacy of the human mind. The idea is well expressed by President Hyde:

"There is a way of looking at our poverty, our plainness of feature, our lack of mental brilliancy, our humble social estate, our unpopularity, our physical ailments, which, instead of making us miserable, will make us modest, contented, cheerful, serene. The mistakes that we make, the foolish words we say, the unfortunate investments into which we get drawn, the failures we experience, all may be transformed by the Stoic formula into spurs to greater effort and stimulus to wiser deeds in days to come. Simply to shift the emphasis from the dead external fact beyond our control to live option which always presents itself within; and to know that the circumstance that can make us miserable simply does not exist, unless it exists by our own consent within our own minds; this is a lesson well worth spending an hour with the Stoics to learn once for all."

With reference to our self-surrender to universal law, the same author says:

"To know that the universal law is everywhere, and that its will may in every circumstance be done; to measure the petty perturbations of our little lives by the vast orbits of natural forces moving according to beneficent and unchanging law; when we come out of the exciting political meeting, or the roar of the stock-exchange, to look up at the calm stars and the tranquil skies and hear them say to us, 'So hot, my little man.' This elevation of our individual lives by the reverent contemplation of the universe and its unswerving laws is something which we may all learn with profit from the old Stoic masters. Business, housekeeping, school-teaching, professional life, politics, society, would all be more noble and dignified if we could bring to them every now and then a touch of this Stoic strength and calm."

III. *Follow the golden mean.* "Nothing in excess." This is the rule of moderation. Our common word "normal" expresses the idea. It is the third of the great Greek precepts which have stood the test of time, and it is as vital as it is simple. A few years ago a university president made the announcement that many students were dying of starvation. They were brain workers and lived on inadequate food, which did not supply their needs of nutrition. They lost vitality and fell a prey to the common diseases. It is a still more common reproach that we overeat. The golden mean in eating is to eat just enough, not too little, and not too much. So, in intellectual life, seek knowledge in a rational way. One of the saddest sights on a college campus is a haggard, nervous wreck in the senior class who has gone to excess in the search for wisdom. The other extreme is more notorious. The rule of moderation means that we shall not be one-sided. The student who is merely an athlete is no farther from the normal than he who wholly neglects the body in the exercise of his mind. Both go to excess.

Similarly, there are some who are in danger of becoming social dolls, and others in danger of becoming moral prigs. One loses himself completely in the pursuit of an art and unfits himself for all other pursuits. Examples abound of religious fanatics who, although intensely religious, live a life unfit both for this world and for the next. On the other hand, the waste of our special talents by neglect is yet more common.

As plain bread is the staff of life, so the homely virtue "moderation" in its psychological aspect becomes the mainstay of a sound mind. But, as it is easier to neglect our powers than to overstrain them, so we need more the injunction "not too little" than the easier "not too much."

IV. *Cultivate repose.* When visiting this country a few years ago, Dr. Clouston, the eminent Scotch physician, as quoted by James, said: "You

Americans wear too much expression on your faces. You are living like an army with all its reserves engaged in action. . . . This thing in you gives me a sense of insecurity, and you ought somehow to tone yourselves down. You really do carry too much expression, you take too intensely the trivial moments of life." To which the retort was made: "But what intelligence it shows! How different from the stolid cheeks, the codfish eyes, the slow, inanimate demeanor we have been seeing in the British Isles!" Even if we join in the retort, we must admit that there is a national danger that lurks in the form of a charm. It has been called a "bottled lightning character"—quick, anxious, responsive, vivacious, effective, charming, but not healthy. We love it and we like to live it, but it is not conducive to longevity. This hurry and flurry has been regarded as a disease called "Americanitis." The European has supreme contempt for it. He takes time for the great things in life, and in this respect sets us an example of repose. The American student is like a hot-house rose; the European student is like a garden rose.

The essence of the power of reasoning is deliberation—the ability to review calmly the premises in all their relations. The rôle of falsehood in politics, religion, and science is often explained by the absence of this repose. Crimes, wars, and countless curses and sufferings are often traceable to lack of repose on the part of the individual or the social group. Logic, justice, art, and religion all demand this quality of poise, balance, and repose.

V. *Be buoyant.* There are two prominent families in the world—the Glads and the Blues—according to Mr. McCutcheon. The Glads are healthy minded and the Blues are sick. Both parties act systematically, on principle, and from habit. Mr. Blue sees the evil in life; Mr. Glad sees the good. Mr. Blue predicts dire events and revels in the prospects of their coming; Mr. Glad says, "Never trouble trouble until trouble troubles you."

Grouchiness is a disease of which there are two varieties, the acute and the chronic. The acute is sudden and of short duration, and the reaction is often beneficial. The chronic type is progressive; it gets worse and worse. Its bodily basis is a physiological habit. There is but little hope of recovery, because it soon develops complexes with other diseases. It is generally recognized by the presence of a delusion to the effect that the environment is bad. This delusion is essentially an external projection of the bad habits of the patient.

Cheerfulness, on the other hand, as a hygienic principle, lends color to life. It is contagious: a cheerful word about the weather at the breakfast table improves the digestion, and the improved digestion leads to a more buoyant appreciation of ourselves, and others, and of the world. There is a little book called "Menti-culture" in which the author suggests that there are two roots of all evil. These two roots are worry and anger; eradicate worry and anger and you will be happy and good. That is too good to be true; and yet it contains a fundamental truth, worthy of practice.

The buoyant are in the long run serious-minded, but there is an air of good humor about them. If it shouldn't go very well, it will go pretty well anyhow; and, at the worst, there is Mark Twain's advice: "If at first you don't succeed, fail, fail again." The joy of living is the surest sign of mental health, and is, in turn, a cause and condition of health.

VI. *Plan to conserve your energies.* The foregoing chapter was devoted to a statement of some of the principles of conservation of human energy. I return to the significance of deliberate forethought in the conservation of mental health.

A moment's reflection often saves hours of labor and pain. Apart from the simple plea, "think before you act," there is the larger plea, "have a plan of life," and the yet larger plea, "let one generation plan for another."

Forethought on the basis of scientific knowledge in medicine is stamping out cholera, malaria, typhoid fever, smallpox, consumption, and many other dreaded diseases of the body. Although more difficult, scientific forethought by the individual and society will in the near future very materially reduce the dreaded mental diseases, such as epilepsy, idiocy, imbecility, and insanity, by precautionary measures. For these are no longer regarded as scourges of blind fate, but are known to be due to natural and traceable causes, explicable in scientific terms, and often preventable.

The possibility of dealing successfully with these grossest types of disease is proof that the countless lesser human ills are being brought under scientific check; and the lesser ills are the more significant because they are so many and so common. We are and should be more concerned about the warding off of inceptive nervousness, for example, than of insanity.

Modern biological experiments in inheritance have demonstrated the possibility of preventing deterioration, eradicating congenital weaknesses, improving the species, and in other ways modifying animals. Horses, chickens, cats, and dogs are being improved systematically under the directing fore-thought of the breeder, and in such transformations in animals a mental trait may be quite as radically modified as a physical trait.

The coming science of eugenics is making a survey of the principles of inheritance applicable to human life. It is taking an inventory of the forces in the environment that make for weal or for woe of man, and is tracing them back to their sources, which are fast being put under control. Eugenics is not only the science of being well-born, but also the science of well-being—not only of physical, but yet more significantly of mental well-being. With a common purpose preventive medicine affects the home, the school, and the civic organization, enlightens the individual and society in regard to private and public sanitation, and concentrates forces of economic, moral, and religious institutions in the common struggle for the one great goal —health.

"Scientific management" is the watchword of the day. The efficiency expert is reaching out into all vocations, from the simplest and lowest physical labor up to the most complicated intellectual effort, showing how by systematic planning we can simplify processes, reduce the amount of effort necessary, and increase the output to an astonishingly great extent. His ideas are practical. Leaders in industry, education, and government find that it pays to have things done in the best way.

Here, then, are three great movements looking toward the increase of human efficiency; namely, preventive medicine, eugenics, and scientific management. More has been done in all of these in the last decade than in the century before. In the light of these facts the generation of to-day is living in a new world of possibilities and responsibilities. The present awakening of civic consciousness and conscience moves man to have regard not only for his own immediate personal well-being, both present and future, but also for that of his neighbor; and the whole world is now one neighborhood.

Conserve your energies, not by a blind fretting over the amelioration of ills of the moment, but by taking hold of the agencies of modern discovery in deliberate and far-sighted self-control.

VII. *Be objective-minded.* It is well enough to say "Be happy," and to wish to be happy and joyful; but, as there is no golden road to success, there is no golden road to happiness. Yet, one of the secrets of success is found in this rule, "be objective-minded."

To develop a healthy intellect do not set yourself logical drill exercises for the mere sake of development, but seek truth, and in that very seeking you will acquire a mastery of intellectual powers. To get social power do not fret over how much you can get for yourself out of the social world nor worry about the formalities of the getting, but seek some definite and immediate end. To get moral power do not walk about with an ill-adjusted conscience; seek out the good and pursue it, and evil will fall by the way. To refine your æsthetic sentiments look for beauty in art and nature and absorb the beauty that is in these objects. Live in the concrete and real present.

The objective-minded person is positive; the subjective-minded person is negative. The negative man has to spend his life in misery trying to ward off evil, trying to get out of trouble, trying to obey the law, ever on the defensive; the best that can be said of him is that he has done no harm. The positive, objective-minded man does not worry about how to be good, how to be true, how to be intellectual, artistic, and religious, but he does something; he forgets self and becomes engrossed in present opportunities. Contrast this positive, objective-minded man with the miserable writhing of the negative, subjective-minded man who wastes life's single opportunity in fear and self-defense.

We may say: Eat for the pleasure of eating;

work for the pleasure of working; seek for the pleasure of seeking; be social for the joy that society gives you; do right for the love of right; revel in the charms of beauty and luxury which surround you, live for the higher life because that is your real life.

VIII. *Play.* Play is a preparation for life, and a means for the realization of life. Without play there can be no healthy mental development or realization of life. This principle has been discussed in an earlier chapter; its conclusions are here relevant.

IX. *Be generous.* The wholesome objective-mindedness of play leads naturally to generosity. Be generous! The healthy-minded are generous givers. An instructor in Yale University gave to a needy man the only pair of mittens he possessed, and then carried his own hands in his pockets for the rest of the winter. That was a generous act, but insignificant as compared with the generosity he showed me and hundreds of other young men who came under his influence. He gave us neither bread nor mittens, but he helped to awaken the better self within our breasts; he was an inspiration to us; he gave us himself; and he did it all unconsciously. If we should thank him to-day he would probably say, "When did I give you this, or that?"

If you were to distinguish yourself for generosity according to your means in your city to-day you would probably be expected to give X dollars to the associated charities, Y dollars to the library fund, Z dollars to the park association—most worthy causes, but all dollars or the equivalent. We seldom think of generosity except in terms of dollars.

Upon due reflection we all share a higher conception of generosity. It consists in giving wisely more than is required of us. There are two principles that may aid in gaining a true idea of generosity; the first is the common-sense principle that you can only give of what you have; and the other is the divine principle: Whatsoever you would that men should do unto you, that do you also unto them. That is, we should give of what we have according to the measure that we would have others mete out to us.

At a very conservative estimate we are at least bodily beings, social beings, intellectual beings, moral beings, æsthetic beings, and religious beings. These beings are true possessions. Generosity may be applied to all possessions: to bread and mittens, to knowledge, to social worth and position, to moral goodness, to appreciation of the beautiful, and to true religion. Each gives what he has.

"That do ye even so unto them," therefore, must include at least this: to show generosity according as we have the means that pertain to the sustenance, protection, development, and rest of the body; the power to think in freedom, and knowledge of the intellectual self; those traits and possessions which constitute a good name and make us socially desirable, useful, and happy; moral integrity, good habits, practical wisdom, and stability of the moral self; that refinement of sensibility and feeling which constitutes the power and essence of the æsthetic self; and a progressive and deepening love, trust, and consecration to God.

The healthy mind is generous. The sick soul is ungenerous. The ungenerosity of the sick soul is shown in many limitations. Intellectually it may be empty-headedness, niggardliness, deceit in any and all forms; morally it may be hatred, malice, vulgarity, sentimentalism, irreverence, remorse. It has been said that the result of education is acquisition of the ability to put yourself in the place of another; that is, to be broad, full of resources, and sympathies. A wholesome education makes a man generous. Spiritual generosity is the absolute *sine qua non* of spiritual growth. In this, more than in material things, generosity enricheth the giver. Service is the key to life. There is no place for the selfish, self-centered, self-seeking individual in a happy family. The same is true in some degree of our social organizations. The selfish soul is ungenerous and must pine away in his own misery, wealthy but a miser, strong but a coward, learned but a fool, gloating in luxury but despicable.

X. *Have ideals*. Be a hero-worshiper. Reflection upon ideals tends to express the ideals in life. You look up to heroes and ideals and thereby give an upward tendency to your whole existence. The mind feeds upon its environment; and this environment is more essentially mental than material. Your mind is full of what you see, hear, feel, touch, and taste; but what the sights, sounds, pressures, odors, and tastes shall mean to you depends upon the more or less clearly recognized ideals; indeed, everything in the mind tends to express itself in accord with the character of the ideal in mind. Therefore, to control conduct we should control the sources upon which the mind feeds, and recognize that the mind develops in the pattern of its ideal. Do you seek mental health? Then permit it to shape itself on your ideal of health. Let your mind be filled with the beauty of literature and art, the charms of noble science and philosophy, the

10   127

light of common sense, the inspiration of noble associates; fix your eye upon the concrete embodiments of these, and they will be reflected in your life.

Observe, in conclusion, how the living of one ideal leads in turn to the living of another. Knowledge of self leads to self-control; self-control leads to moderation; moderation leads to poise; poise takes one out of the subjective brooding and makes one objective-minded; objective-mindedness enhances the power of forethought with reference to the conservation of energy; conservation of energy leads to play; play leads to generosity and altruism; and generosity leads to the appreciation of ideals.

CHAPTER V

MENTAL LAW

Since the general aim in this book is to set forth the applications of psychology, I shall limit the present chapter to the presentation of a few general principles, which underlie specific laws of mental behavior, in their immediate bearing upon daily life. The following chapter will then be devoted to a single intensive illustration of a series of mental laws, laws of illusion.

Psychology, the study of mental nature, aims to describe and explain mental processes. It aims to know how we think, feel, and will; how we learn and forget; how we grow and decay mentally; how we perceive, remember, think, love, hate, fear, adore, obey, desire, choose, wish, and will—even how we dream or act absent-mindedly and unconsciously. The study of these mental processes has become experimental and scientific with the recognition of mental processes as phenomena in nature, subject to the domain of natural law. Thus considered, psychology is an organized search for the laws of mental nature. These laws, like the laws in the physical sciences, are warranted hypotheses based upon a limited number of observed facts; they serve for economy of effort in thought and expression; they summarize, formulate, and explain data; they support principles of application.

The human brain is a microcosm, a small universe, no less wonderful than the macrocosm of the stellar universe, no less complex in organization. It has been estimated that there are about nine thousand million cells in the central nervous system of man. Each one of these is an organism complete in itself, with the power of generating, storing, and distributing nervous energy. Each one is made up of millions of molecules arranged in a purposive and orderly fashion, and each molecule, the modern physicist tells us, is itself as highly organized and complex in structure as a modern man-of-war; and, in this microcosm, we believe that not a molecule moves except in accordance with natural law.

This picture of the nervous organization of the brain serves the psychologist to suggest the complexity of the mental life, for there is a correspondence between the mental processes and the neural processes. The stream of mental life, no less complex than its material substratum, is made up of impressions, stored, adapted, elaborated, fused, transformed, and expressed—all in accord with mental law.

In times past "natural" has often been thought to mean "material," and the laws of nature have accordingly been monopolized by the material sciences. But now we regard mental phenomena no less than physical phenomena as facts in nature. Believing that mental operations are natural as opposed to either the supernatural or the nonexistent, we regard our nature as a psycho-physical nature; we live in a mental environment as truly as we live in a physical environment.

The opinions of men of science differ widely on this subject. I shall present a few general principles, which set forth a point of view, and for that purpose submit the following propositions: (1) The principle of retention: every sense impression tends to leave a trace; (2) the principle of expression: every mental process tends toward expression; (3) the principle of reception: every new experience is limited by previous experiences; (4) the principle of reproduction: every mental process tends to recur according to law; (5) the principle of unification: mental development tends toward automatism. I shall not attempt to prove these propositions, but shall merely try to indicate something of the scope and significance of their operation in our daily life.

EVERY SENSE-IMPRESSION LEAVES A TRACE

Every impression made through the sense organs tends to leave a trace. The emphasis is upon the word "every"; and this emphasis becomes more significant when we recognize the number and variety of such impressions. There are obviously more than the "five" senses of man, commonly recognized. We have at least nine or ten, and these newly discovered senses play no small rôle. Thus, without the so-called sixth sense, the muscle sense, technically known as the kinæsthetic sense, or the sense of strain, we would be helpless in every effort to stand, walk, talk, or eat. Every muscle that can be moved at will is guided on the basis of a complex system of incoming messages, which report position, weight, strain, resistance, and movement in terms of the muscles in action. So simple a movement as carrying a bit of bread to the mouth with the fingers involves a complicated chain of adjustments of arm, wrist, hand, fingers, eyes, neck, lips, and tongue. Each progressive change in the series of coördinated adjustments of all these sets of muscles is based upon a full series of incoming messages through the muscle-sense relating to the position and movement of the parts. This wonderful system of communication with the muscles has been perfected to such a high degree that it is almost self-acting. We serve ourselves repeatedly by such movements without particular effort, and yet with such accuracy that a misguided movement is very unusual. The impressions through the muscle-sense serve their purpose faithfully. So in each of the lower senses there are systems upon systems of impressions that, by virtue of their excellent adaptation, pass without notice. In the higher senses this is true on a larger scale. The number and complexity of the impressions which may be involved in such an act, for example, as looking at a passing person for one second are astonishingly great.

One reason for the late recognition of these hidden senses lies in the fact that they are so firmly organized and well adjusted that impressions from them seldom disturb or tax consciousness. The sense of equilibrium is a case in point. Only a part of the inner mechanism within which the organ of hearing is situated serves the purpose of hearing; closely connected with it is the organ of the sense of equilibrium. There is in each ear a system of canals acting on the principle of a spirit level, with one such level for each of the three dimensions of space. The balancing of the body, as in sitting, standing, or moving, is governed in part by the registration of balance or orientation through these levels. Yet all sober and sound persons make this intricate adjustment in the ordinary maintenance of position without any marked consciousness of balancing.

The qualifying term "every" gets its largest significance when the principle is stated exclusively from the neural point of view. The principle then applies not only to those sensory nerve-impulses which result in conscious experience, but also to the much larger mass of sensory nerve-impulses that result in subconscious impressions, and may be extended to the sensory nerve-impulses that are not known to have any direct mental correlates. The principle stated in terms of the nervous system does not detract from its significance as a psycho-physic law; for psychology assumes a far-reaching correlation between the sensory mental processes and the sensory neural processes. Just how far downward toward the purely physiological this parallelism extends is uncertain.

Theoretically, every sense impression regardless of its strength or frequency leaves a trace. The meaning of this statement may be made clear by an analogy. An earthquake disturbs a body of water violently; a ship plying at surface changes its distribution; a single drop falling makes an impression, however small, and the continued falling of drop after drop causes great changes in the level and distribution of the water, but no drop disappears without a trace. Just so the conscious, strong, and relevant impressions make marked changes in the psycho-physic organism; but the stream of processes in this organism is made up in large part of merged "drops," the countless faint impressions, each of which, though losing its identity, enters into the composition and cumulative flow of the ever-changing stream.

Sentience, affection, skill, and character all rest upon an incomparably broader foundation of fact than that of the sum total of consciously experienced impressions. We are seldom judged by our intentions or the attitudes we strike; we are judged by the attitudes in which we are least concerned with the effect we are to produce. When we judge a man we seldom develop a rational opinion of him from an indifferent point of view; on the contrary, we first fall into an attitude toward him, and then proceed to picture him to ourselves from that point of view, usually without being aware of the existing bent of mind or of the impressions which caused it. This is true not only in friendships and aversions, but as well in our rich life of feeling-attitudes toward objects, events, ideas, and ideals in life. The countless inflowing impressions have left their traces, which exist as forces or tendencies; our attitudes are in large part the resultants of such forces.

The practical significance of this principle is far-reaching and plain. If you were to write an essay on "The borrowed elements of my personality," in which you trace the origin and course of development of some little specific characteristic of yourself which you regard as distinctly your own and original with yourself (such as a certain stage in a smile, an accent, or the loop of the "y" in your writing, if it be peculiarly your own) you might be disillusioned. If the analysis is made searching you are likely to find an "original" outside of yourself which you have perhaps adopted in unconscious imitation. This original has had a checkered career as a part of you; it has been the butt of circumstances and has been modified by many influences from within and from without. Treat other elements of your most spontaneous and personal characteristics in the same way and you will gain appreciation for the idea that the countless impressions which pour in upon us gradually, though often slowly and by irregular stages, work themselves into the warp and woof of our personal character.

At the present moment your consciousness is properly centered upon the reading of this chapter or upon some reflections suggested by it. But at this very time there is a mass of visual, auditory, taste, smell, temperature, strain, pain, and equilibrium sensations pressing in upon you. Every one leaves a trace. You feel with compunction that your mind is wandering. There is a fleeting array of undifferentiated ideas and impressions passing through you. Every one leaves a trace; it changes the growing mind so that the mental content is different from what it would have been if any one of these impressions had not occurred.

It is one of the great blessings of nature that so few of these traces reach consciousness in the act of impression, and that still fewer are ever consciously recalled as individual impressions. Rationality, endurance, discreet cognition, and action rest upon the fact that consciousness is selective, personal, purposive, and of particular things. And, again, it is fortunate that this elimination is automatic and therefore easy and effective. If we should be conscious of all impressions strong enough to reach consciousness in a given hour we should become mentally wrecked. So sensitive is our psycho-physical organism that it registers everything, and so wonderfully are we organized that we can utilize stored-up experience with but slight expenditure of conscious effort.

EVERY MENTAL PROCESS TENDS TOWARD EXPRESSION

All mental life is motor. The flow of the stream of mental life is all in one direction, the course being represented by the three large stages, reception, elaboration, and expression. No matter at what stage or level a mental process may arise it always tends toward expression. This may be observed in such a common momentary act as that of seeing and greeting a friend. I chance upon a friend in a throng, and we immediately shake hands. Though brief, that act involves a rushing stream of consciousness—sensations, perceptions, images, ideas, feelings, and volitions; each process with its rich and complicated variations is a part of the same stream, and the stream flows on in the direction of action. Our sense impressions, memories, thoughts, feelings, impulses, and deliberations all tend to result in action. This is but the outward evidence of the fact that the purpose of consciousness is to mediate adjustment.

All thought is inceptive action. This may be demonstrated and measured. If we attach a delicate registering instrument to the throat of a person and ask him to speak a sentence, we may obtain a graphic record of certain movements of the vocal organs in the speaking; if, under the same circumstances, we let him merely whisper the same sentence we get a graphic record like the former, only less bold; and if then we let him merely think, *i. e.,* recite the sentence mentally, we again get a similar graphic record, though very much fainter than in the other two cases: even in the mere thinking the vocal organs made inceptive movements to express the words.

Our actions reflect our minds. One of the best illustrations of this is furnished by "mind-reading." A friend of mine of extraordinary intelligence and self-control consulted a palmist. Within ten minutes of the beginning of the sitting—in addition to a number of self-evident facts—he was told the following specific facts: "You are a married man." "You have three children." "Your wife has had one miscarriage." "You have crossed the ocean three times." "You have made much money, but you made an unfortunate investment and sustained a heavy financial loss in the month of November"; all of which was entirely true. The sitter had not spoken either to assent or dissent. He had been sitting with downcast eyes and had taken every precaution to be noncommittal. Yet, I have not the slightest doubt that the medium got all this information from the sitter on the spot, and without telepathy. The medium is an artist whose principal ingenuity consists in covered talk which draws from the sitter unconscious expression of affirmation or denial; and the apparently meaningless "patter" of the medium is really a continuous chain of questions which the sitter answers by automatic reactions which the ingenious medium has learned to interpret.

No person can look at a lewd picture, hear debasing words, or think depraved thoughts without having this tinge the attitudes of his life. By that I do not mean that a settlement worker, for example, cannot work among the fallen and stricken without becoming debased. On the contrary, all the evil which she sees enlightens her in regard to the needs of the wretched and may move her to sacrifice her life for them. In fact, like the surgeon who looks upon a wound under control as a beautiful wound, this worker may feel that the slums constitute a most promising field for rich returns, and that to draw humanity from the depths of suffering and despair is a great privilege. Yet, in such a reaction the tinge may be traceable, for example, in the callousness of professional attitude. Likewise daily contact with the beauty of nature, or with works of art, or noble deeds, will invariably result in some sort of reflection of the traces of these in the character of the mind, even though it results in an attitude of apparent indifference.

Every secret thought tends to be expressed. Shamming is notoriously a failure. Try to keep a secret. It seems to be in the way. Other ideas have to take circuitous routes to keep clear of it. It has to be fortified. Protecting ideas have to be set up around it. All this going around and fortifying is an expression of the secret. Who has not inadvertently said just the thing that he desired most to conceal? It is said that the word "glad" often creeps in to take the place of the word "sorry" in notes of regret. The present movement in psychotherapy called psychanalysis rests upon this law. An hysterical patient comes to a physician for treatment. To discover the source of the hysterical condition the physician uses a chronoscope, by means of which he measures in hundredths of a second the time of response of the patient to selected words. He soon discovers words related to the cause of the trouble and, by following these significant words logically, he can diagnose the trouble.

The current movement in the psychology of testimony, as applied to the testimony of criminals, rests upon the same principle. We recently tried a case of this type of mind-reading in the psychological laboratory. An experimental case was devised in which the accused person was either guilty or not guilty of doing a certain thing. The students who acted as psychological judges were not previously trained in this particular experiment, yet in nineteen cases out of twenty-one they gave a correct judgment; and this judgment was based entirely upon the quickness and the nature of the response which the accused made to a few words selected for the purpose.

Even our dreams express themselves. One day I remarked at the dinner table that this is the celery season and that the celery is very good this year. It is especially good for the children, and I suggested that we have it as frequently as possible. The following day when I came to the dinner table and saw the celery it came to me like a flash that the reason that I had recommended the celery the day before lay in the fact that, during the previous night, I had dreamed of seeing a farmer driving into town with a hayrack-load of the most luscious celery. Yet, the day before, when I spoke of the celery crop as being good, I had no specific image in mind and did not remember having dreamed about it.

Our dream life expresses itself constantly and very effectively in our daily life, but we seldom discover the fact. We may go further and say that no matter whether a dream is ever remembered or not—known or unknown—the dream has effect upon the waking life. The same is true of daydreams, reveries, mind-wanderings, mental blanks, so-called confusions, and idlings.

It has been said that a child is a bundle of possibilities; woman is a bundle of inconsistencies; and man is—a bigger bundle of inconsistencies. Neglecting the comparison, this is true. Man is his character. Character is only the inner view of conduct. Conduct is the realization of a vast number of possibilities; only a few of these realizations are guided by conscious and consistent choice. The bulk of conduct is unconscious expression of the psycho-physical constitution. For, every impression leaves a trace and every trace has its effect, however infinitesimally small, in the ever-changing stream of mental life.

To influence conduct we must modify the mental content so as to favor certain possibilities and check others. A man who wishes to change the flow in a waterfall does not get in under the fall and beat the water back, nor does he increase the flow by pressing at the fall. He goes up the stream and, if he wishes to increase the flow, he throws up dykes and gathers in more sources. If he wishes to decrease the flow he diverts a part of the stream from the regular channel some distance above the falls. Recognizing this fundamental principle of expression, the true educator will proceed in the same way in controlling the stream of mental life.

I have taken pains to emphasize the effect of the little known and the little noticed mental process for two reasons. In the first place, the fact that the clearly conscious and prominent mental processes, such as joy, fear, and reflection, result in expression is generally known and recognized; and, in the second place, these lower processes are infinitely more numerous than the higher, so that they become important by reason of their massiveness; they constitute the body of the stream from which conduct flows.

EVERY NEW EXPERIENCE IS LIMITED BY PREVIOUS EXPERIENCE

Experience is interpretation. The growing mind is not like the clay, which is modeled from without.

To experience a thing is to give meaning to a sign of that thing. The seeing of a flower is in a real sense a self-expression of the seeing person. What the flower shall be to him depends upon what he is. The impression from without is merely a signal or a cue upon which the mind builds a percept in accord with its own character. When the flower is remembered there is no reinstatement of the original percept; the mind constructs afresh an image which is built on the pattern of the original percept of the flower, but this memory-image differs from the original percept according to the interests of the person who remembers it. Even sensation is not mere impression; because every sensory experience is dependent upon attention for its intensity and clearness, and its effectiveness depends most vitally upon the make-up of the mind to which it owes its existence and of which it becomes a part. This principle of interpretation applies not only to conscious reactions, but in a limited sense also to the accessions to the lower mental levels, below the threshold of consciousness.

Experience is selective interpretation. A given object may leave countless varieties of meaning, depending upon the bent of mind of the interpreter. A flower may be to the farmer a weed which must be killed to keep it from going to seed; to the manufacturer of perfumes a fragrant material which must be converted into an essential oil; to the botanist, a specimen of a new species of which every part, including leaves, stem, and roots, must be preserved as evidence; to the artist, a bit of color tint which his brush must transfer to the portrait on the easel; to the tourist, the emblem of a sentiment which must be lovingly preserved and transmitted to his sweetheart across the waters. In these cases the flower is not only recognized as having different uses, but each person perceives only a limited aspect of the physical flower, and these aspects may all be different. The farmer sees the flower as a part of a mass of flowers in his wheat; the perfumer merely identifies by sight the flower which to him is essentially an odor; the botanist sees the form of the serration of the leaves and the shape of the container of the pollen; the artist's eye is caught by the exquisite tint near the tip of a petal which he has long idealized as a life-color; while the tourist sees, through the symmetry, grace, purity, and brilliance of the flower, the ideal of his heart, and the presence of this ideal takes away the imperfections of the real flower.

Selective interpretation in experience is narrowing. No two individuals have inherited the same kind or extent of equipment from the past. This cleavage of individual difference rapidly broadens with the evolving personal interests. The innate bent or limitation of the mind increases the effect of the narrowing influence of selective interpretation. Experience soon tends to set us in fixed ruts which in their adverse aspects take the form of bias, prejudice, callousness, and ill-founded conviction. There is not a developed mind which does not suffer from this tendency in some respect. The good lady was right when she observed that "all people are a little queer, except thee and me, and thee is a little queer, too." As James says, we are all old fogies in our attitudes toward some things, even in early childhood. I have known persons who were such old fogies as to think that they had no prejudices. But, as stubbornness is merely an aberration from the high moral quality of firmness, so prejudice and bias are merely more or less ill-advised variants of the principle of specialization, which is a prime condition of efficiency and achievement.

This principle is generally known as the principle of apperception. It designates the synthetic or meaning-giving activity of the mind in new experience, and conveys the idea that every mental development is an outgrowth from previous development of the mind, and is therefore limited by such previous development. The evidence of this fact is one of the charms in the observation of the child, and may be noticed throughout all the stages of growth, even in the learning processes of the mature adult. The principle has become a cornerstone in the foundation of educational theory. Among other principles of practice in teaching derived from it are the following: (1) Organize the method and content of instruction so that the new experience shall stand in effective relationship to previous experience and be a natural outgrowth from it; (2) adapt the content and the method of the instruction progressively to the stages in the development of the child; and (3) adapt the content of the educational appeal to the natural capacity and bent of mind of the individual. These three rules may be reduced to one: adapt the instruction to the individual.

According to the first of these three rules there should be a natural sequence in subjects, as is clearly demanded in mathematics; a new concept should be illustrated and explained in terms of old and familiar concepts; and the child should be led into new interests through existing interests. The second rule has been intimately associated with the idea that the child passes in epitome through the fundamental stages of development that the species has passed through in its evolution. It recognizes that characteristic instincts and impulses appear in a fairly recognized order in the growth of the child, and demands that instruction shall be so planned that it shall take advantage of the progressive outcropping of characteristic interest, tendencies, and capacities of the growing mind. It would say, first find the natural capacities and talents of the individual; then make the education fit the individual. For it is essential that the new experience shall be such as to appeal to the individual and be within his grasp, if it is to be construed efficiently. Make a boy feel that he is doing something which he is fit to do and loves to do, and by which he is sure to profit and be rewarded, and you need not worry about temptations, idleness, waywardness, crime, and disgrace. To violate this law is to attempt to force the growing mind into a form unsuited to it. Its wise and sympathetic application gives the mind of exceptional promise a fair chance.

MENTAL PROCESSES RECUR ACCORDING TO NATURAL LAW

All the reproductive processes, such as habit, memory, and imagination, and the more complex processes, such as conception, judgment, and reasoning, follow certain fundamental laws in common. These we call the laws of association. When we profit by experience, when we acquire skill through practice, when we orient ourselves in the past, we find that it is always through the operation of a system of laws of association.

When we examine these laws we find that they may be reduced to three large groups. These are (1) contiguity: events which have occurred together tend to recur together; (2) similarity: each experience tends to call up similar experiences; and (3) contrast: things and events suggest their opposites. Contrast is merely the obverse of similarity; these two are therefore frequently classified as one. Contiguity is the simplest type and the commonest; similarity, the highest; and contrast, the most effective, when used sparingly.

To illustrate, take the matter of impressing the truth: "Thou shalt not steal." The dog carries the master's dinner basket and does not lunch upon it, because he has formed the association between the image of the thing-to-be-carried-and-not-eaten and some word or act forbidding him to eat. These two experiences have occurred together a sufficient number of times and the dog is faithful merely because the principle of contiguity is strong enough to guide him. Although infants and adults may learn the commandment within its wide ramifications and obey it similarly by simply following the association of contiguity, they early tend to recognize another bond—the principle of similarity. The developed mind tends to use the principle of similarity. From "thou shalt not steal this and this" it acquires the ability to see the similarity of cases. The whole system of rational conduct rests upon the principle of similarity. All classification is simply the application of the principle of similarity; therefore science is essentially an elaboration on the principle of similarity. If emotions are to be awakened clear experiences of contrast are helpful. The learner sets off on one side, for example, the consequences of stealing and, on the other side, the consequences of not stealing. By this use of the principle of contrast the acquisitions through the principles of contiguity and similarity may be fortified.

In this very use of the primary laws we discover the action of numerous secondary laws. The primary laws are qualitative; the secondary laws are quantitative. The primary laws express the kind of relationship that may exist; the secondary laws express the conditions which favor these relationships. Familiar illustrations of the secondary or quantitative laws are (1) the law of primacy: other things being equal, the first impression will be the most effective; (2) the law of intensity: other things being equal, the strongest impression will have the greatest effect; (3) the law of duration: other things being equal, the longest continued association will have the greatest effect; (4) the law of repetition: other things being equal, the more frequently the association has been repeated the more effective it will be; (5) the law of exception: other things being equal, the more frequently an association has been broken the weaker it will be; (6) the law of recency: other things being equal, the most recent impression will be the most effective. Then there are certain general principles, such as that of interest: we remember best those facts which we have observed with the keenest interest; the principle of emotional congruity: other things being equal, we remember best those impressions that are congruous with our feelings; that is, we tend to remember happy things when we are happy and sad things when we are sad; and the principle of effort or intention: other things being equal, we remember best that which we have tried to remember.

Association is not a specific mental process in itself; it is the bond of connection which exists between all elements of mental content. Perception, imagination, feeling, and actions are mental processes; association is the internal coördinating mechanism within and among them. Reproduction by the principle of association is present in all mental life, even in "simple" sensations; for, even in these the instinctive, blind, associative tendencies are undoubtedly at work moulding the impression.

Association, like the principle of chemical affinity in the physical world, holds the fusions of elements together, and explains their behavior in a fundamental way. As we have roots and trunks of trees, so we have sensations, images, and thoughts in the mind undergoing growth, being alive, and being made over, and put to use through the operation of natural law. What the laws of chemical affinity are to the world of matter, the laws of association are to the world of mind. As the physicist, the chemist, and the biologist work through, explain by, and believe implicitly in the laws which govern the combination, evolution, and fixity of physical compounds, so the psychologist works through, explains by, and believes implicitly in such laws as the laws of association in the complex of mental life.

MENTAL DEVELOPMENT TENDS TOWARD AUTOMATISM

As we grow we acquire more and more power to do things automatically. The most effective freedom of action is the automatic. If you try to drive a nail by guiding your arm consciously you may come to grief. How do you play the piano as long as you have to think this bar, this note, this finger, this key? You do not profess to play until the movements are automatic. The boy who is just learning to raise his hat to ladies and elders often does it laboriously, grudgingly, and awkwardly. No one is polite unless he is polite by his very nature. What kind of man would I be if, before every assertion, I had to stop and deliberate: Shall I tell a lie or shall I tell the truth? To what extent shall I tell the truth? No one is trustworthy until the right of way is given to truth automatically. The idea of telling the truth is so deeply ingrained in our nature and has suffered so few violations that we need pay no attention to that matter in ordinary events. In the same manner habits of attention, habits of thinking conscientiously, habits of purity, habits of tenderness, habits of appreciation, habits of obedience, habits of revenge, in short, those capacities and acquisitions which give us strong and effective characters are essentially automatic.

The highest character consists in a completely fashioned will. But a completely fashioned will, a perfect automatism, is not within our reach. Our supreme attainment and therefore our immediate goal is not the perfect mind, but the free mind, and herein lies the principal function of consciousness.

Consciousness and freedom are temporary affairs which appear only at points of new adjustment. When the boy is to learn to raise his hat he should be free to acquire the feeling that the raising of the hat is a sign of good breeding; that it is an honor to himself and to the person greeted; that it gives a delightful feeling of satisfaction in power and self-mastery; that it goes well with a smile and a compliment; that it brings returns; that it is a means of relieving pent-up energies by knowing how to dispose of the hands; that he can thereby actually express individually his appreciation of the person greeted; that raising the hat is not that trifling physical act alone, but, when properly done, is the entering of one mind into relation with another; that this little act of manners is a part of the making of the man; that if he does this with all his heart he will acquire the power to do greater things with the same ease. This implies ability to hesitate, and to gauge the situation in his own mind; it means willingness to cope with instinctive cravings; it means willingness to fight single-handed for personal adjustment. All this tends to throw him into an attitude of profoundest consciousness of this act for the time being. At this beginning of a new adjustment it is well that he should be free to think, feel, and act with the most absorbing consciousness. But, as soon as he has learned to raise his hat, that process should take care of itself, should be automatic, so that the act is performed on every appropriate occasion without hesitation and without consciousness of conflict, but with the fullest richness of significance. Only when the adjustments once made through the most strenuous consciousness are self-acting will his consciousness be free for new operations, for the making of new adjustments.

Richness in well-formed habits is the indispensable foundation of progressively higher orders of freedom. The man who has formed the habits of truthfulness, cleanliness, industry, kindness, appreciation, sympathy, moral integrity, reverence, and hope lives these habits without hesitation and without effort. While he is living the efficient life of this automatized self his consciousness is free to be engaged in the mastering of new situations which, for the time being, demand attention and deliberation. One of the most desirable habits one can acquire is that of keeping his habits plastic. Worship, for example, should be a habit; but this habit should broaden in scope from day to day as the love and power of God are revealed, so that there may be more and more situations which keep the heart attuned in reverent worship.

Our object is so to systematize our life that the commonest, the most vital, and the most efficient responses shall follow by "rule of precedent." He is the best general who commands successfully with the fewest orders and counter-orders. As in a well-organized administration the head of the government determines policies, assumes responsibility, and manages the nation with a few decrees; so consciousness presides over the mental organization by holding itself responsive and responsible, acting upon new situations, and making a few decisions; and life is efficient in so far as the psycho-physic organism is faithfully responsive to the more and more general decrees issued by a dominant, controlling consciousness.

The study of mental law with reference to daily life reveals the meaning, the beauty, and the dignity of our plain and common acts; it explains and interprets much of what is so essentially our nature that it is apt to be taken for granted; it gives us a glimpse into the genesis, the evolution, the goal, the values of our common powers; it gives us the power to plan and govern our daily conduct with feeling and forethought; it tends to make us positive, generous, and optimistic by revealing unsuspected worth in our various selves; it explores and prospects in the mental life, and thus defies the primitive taboo of the soul; and in the name of the dignity and power of mind in the world it proclaims the possession and sovereignty of the mental nature.

CHAPTER VI

LAW IN ILLUSION

To supplement the foregoing chapter, which is apparently composed of assertions without the supporting evidence, the present chapter is devoted to a concrete illustration of the kind of evidence that may be arrayed in support of the dominance of law in mental nature.

It may seem plausible that the plain and reliable processes such as sensation, memory, and association follow law, but less so that the more complex and indirect processes such as illusions, hallucinations, delusions, impulsions, and dreams may be reduced to law and order. Let us therefore take one of the most doubtful cases, illusions, and see whether there is method in such apparently irregular phenomena. If we can substantiate the claim in this extreme instance the case may be regarded as proved. For this purpose we may take the case of normal illusions and select three concrete illustrations of typical situations in daily life; namely, some illusions of the twisted cord, of the silk hat, and of the medicine bottle.

THE TWISTED CORD: ILLUSIONS OF DIRECTION

In order that the reader may begin this chapter with the actual experience of an illusion I shall first present a few pictures which involve what is called the "unit of direction" illusion. This consists of a shift in the apparent shape and direction of figures composed of patterns which in their simplest form suggest a twisted cord.[1]

In Fig. 5 the letters which are outlined by the twisted cord seem to tilt; they are in fact perfectly erect and well balanced, as may be seen by applying a straight-edge. Fig. 6 indicates that the illusion lies mainly in the twisted cord, since it is almost as striking when the plaid pattern is absent. This is corroborated by Fig. 7 which shows that the illusion does not obtain for the plaid alone, without the twisted cord. However, by combining the twisted cord with certain parts of the plaid pattern, as in Fig. 5, the maximum illusion is produced. The illusions in these designs will be enhanced by

[1] Figures 5-17 are reproduced through the courteous consent of the author, Dr. James Frazer, and the publishers of his article on "A New Visual Illusion of Direction" in the British Journal of Psychology, Vol. II, pp. 307 ff.

turning the page so as to look at the patterns from the side.

In Fig. 8a the twisted cord seems to form a continuous spiral, but it really forms a series of concentric circles of which 8b is an exact outline. To verify this apply a pair of dividers and trace the circles.[1]

In Fig. 9 the rings of twisted cords are again perfect circles, which may be proved as in the foregoing figure, but they appear to be quite irregular. Likewise, the rings in Figs. 10, 11, 12, and 13 are perfect circles, although their appearance is very different.

The radiating spokes in Fig. 14 are uniformly spaced at the "hub," but they seem to enter by pairs as wedges. The vertical lines in Fig. 15 are straight and parallel, but they seem to be decidedly bent. The same is true of the columns in Fig. 17, which would not prove a very restful pattern for a fireplace tile.[2] The columns, although straight and made up of perfect parallelograms, seem to topple.

This illusion has been called the "Unit of Di-

[1] A strip of paper with one pin at the center and one tracing the circle will answer the purpose of dividers. If 8b be drawn on tissue paper and laid over 8a, the fact of their coincidence will appear.

[2] A certain firm of tile manufacturers actually offered this as one of their designs for fireplace tiles.

rection" illusion, because, although other motives are involved, the main motive is a tendency to get the direction from each unit of direction singly instead of from the figure as a whole. This is best

Fig. 17

illustrated in Fig. 5, where each separate unit of direction stands out distinctly by itself and is made up of a line joining two blocks. Some such units of direction are shown separately in Fig. 16. All figures are variants upon this same principle, as may be seen by selecting the unit of direction in each figure, down to the last (Fig. 17), in which it consists of two blocks alone indicating the direction. Applying this principle, one can account

Fig. 5

Fig. 6

Fig. 7

Fig. 8a

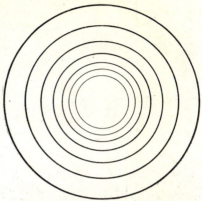

Fig. 8b

Fig. 9

Fig. 10

FIG. 11

FIG. 12

FIG. 13

FIG. 14

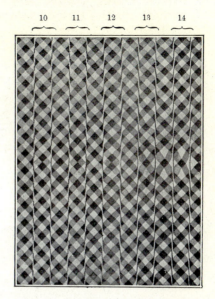

FIG. 15

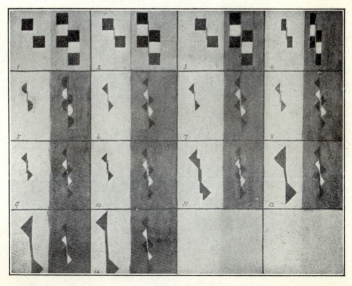

FIG. 16

in large part for all the distortions in the figures. It must, however, be remembered that there are other motives, some favoring and others opposing the appearance of the unit of direction illusion in these figures. The most striking of these is the fact of irradiation which does much to enhance the force of the illusion in Fig. 17.

The fact that this illusion is normal, predictable, and consistent with some law is attested by the fact that, although appreciably diminished in force by knowledge of its nature, the illusion persists and remains irrepressible for all normal persons, no matter how long or how frequently they regard it. Even the few variants of the figures shown suffice to suggest that we do not have far to go to find unit of direction figures, as in prints on fabrics, in pictorial art, or in natural objects.

THE SILK HAT: ILLUSIONS OF SIZE

A visitor in the psychological laboratory asked why it is that a silk hat looks so much taller than it really is. The psychologist replied, "Let us see whether or not it does." The persons present were asked to agree upon a height to which the hat would correspond if it were placed against the wall on the window sill. A point was agreed upon and, when the hat was set up, it fell short of the mark by fully twenty-five per cent of its actual height; that is, they had judged the hat to be higher than it really was. They were then asked to judge in-

FIG. 18

dividually the ratio of the height to the diameter, the diameter being arbitrarily considered ten units, for convenience. The judgment on height ranged from twelve to sixteen units, but measurement showed that the two dimensions were exactly equal. This confirmed the first observation. Thus was demonstrated in a new sense that much of the impression made by the silk hat is mere appearance.

In Fig. 18 the greatest height (front) of the cylinder is equal to the smallest diameter of the top of the crown. The height looks to be about one-fourth greater than the diameter.

This incident was recognized as a good starting point for an investigation. A student took up the problem and made a very extensive series of qualitative and quantitative experiments which required years of work and resulted in a valuable contribution to the science of psychology.[1]

In making measurements we must analyze the situation into its simplest elements and proceed intensively and with one element at a time. Now the main constituent "element" of the hat is a cylinder. So the first general question was, What illusions are involved in the cylinder, and to what extent do these account for the gross illusions found in the hat?

A series of metal cylinders was made, all 114 mm. in diameter, but each varying in length by five millimeters from 69 mm. to 124 mm. In this series a number of observers were required to select, under experimental conditions, that cylinder in which the diameter seemed to be equal to the height. The results varied for different individuals, but on the average a cylinder was selected

---

[1] Mabel Clare Williams, *Normal Illusions in Representative Geometrical Forms.* Univ. of Iowa Studies in Psychology. Vol. III, 1902, pp. 38-139.

whose length was eighteen per cent. shorter than the diameter.[1]

But a portion of this eighteen per cent. is due to the well-known illusion of the vertical. Vertical distances, as compared with horizontal distances, are always overestimated. The squares in the surface of Nos. 2, 9, and 10, appear to be higher than they are wide. To eliminate this factor, the experiment was repeated with the cylinders all presented so that the axis of rotation lay in the horizontal plane, which would be represented by looking at No. 3 from the side of the page. The result showed that there was no marked error; the right cylinder was often selected. This proved that we were dealing with two opposing motives, one tending to lengthen the cylinder, and the other to shorten it, and that in this position they approximately equalize each other. In the first experiment these two motives coöperate, while here they are opposed. Since they practically equalize one another when opposed, we see that they are approximately equal in force—about 9 per cent. This 9 per cent. tallies well with

[1] In this as in all the following quantitative statements I shall use the average, bearing in mind that there are always fluctuations around this average. I would also state once for all that the phrase "other things being equal" should be understood in this chapter wherever the text naturally suggests it.

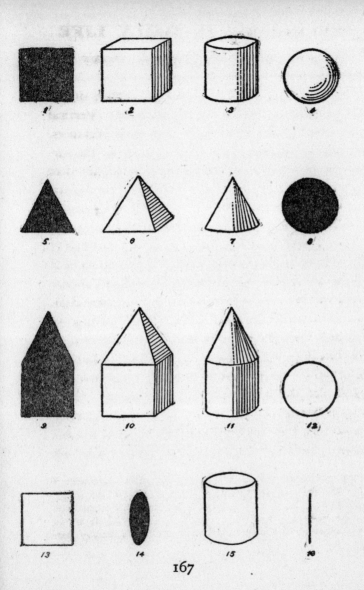

what is generally known as the force of the illusion of the vertical for these conditions. The new illusion we shall call the "Illusion of Cylinder Length," and we may remember that it has about the same force as the well-known illusion of the vertical.

The next step was to get a more direct measurement. The cylinder whose height was equal to its diameter was compared with the horizontal line.[1] The observers were required to select from a series of lines presented singly, under experimental conditions, a horizontal line which seemed to be equal to the height of the cylinder. On the average a line was selected which was more than twenty-five per cent. too long. This proved that the original illusion observed in the hat was essentially inherent in the cylinder; exact measurements on the illusion might now proceed with the cylinder in its simplified and regular shape.

The discrepancy between the second and the third measurements indicates a residuum, probably mean-

[1] In psychological measurements it is customary to take a straight horizontal line of medium length as basal because, so far as we know, this comes nearest to being free from motives for illusion. The other directions and dimensions may be referred to it as a base or norm. Even if our assumption should not be quite correct, this line still serves quite as well as a relative basis of evaluation.

ing that there is some marked illusion in the diameter as well as in the height of the cylinder. Actual measurements revealed an overestimation of the diameter of the cylinder amounting, on the average, to thirteen per cent. If we now add the thirteen per cent. to the eighteen per cent. found in the second experiment, we get a total overestimation of thirty-one per cent. for the height of the cylinder. This tallies well with the results found in the third experiment.

But we must have an explanation of this discovery. Through a series of ingenious, crucial experiments, it was found that this thirteen per cent. of overestimation of the diameter was reducible to two motives for illusion, which were named respectively the "Area-illusion" and the "Volume-illusion," each amounting to about six per cent. by itself, and that these illusions apply to the length as well as to the diameter of the cylinder.

The area illusion may be demonstrated by trying to select a line (No. 16, Fig. 19) equal to the height of one side of the square (No. 1). A line too long by about six per cent. will be selected. The volume illusion may be demonstrated by selecting a square which shall seem equal in width and height to the width and height of the face of the cube

(No. 2). A square too large by about six per cent. will be selected.

This is but the beginning of the procedure. We started out with one well-known illusion, that of the vertical, and so far we have discovered three new illusions; namely, the illusion of cylinder-length, the area-illusion, and the volume-illusion. Let us stop at this stage and recall the steps taken. With the cylinder in the vertical position, the illusion of the vertical adds nine per cent. to the length, the area-illusion six per cent., and the volume-illusion six per cent., making a total of thirty per cent.; and the area-illusion adds six per cent. and the volume-illusion at least six per cent. to the diameter, making a total of twelve per cent.[1] There are a great many other normal illusions involved in the silk hat, but these are the largest factors, and the total result is not much altered by taking other illusions into account because, in the long run, they tend to balance one another, some tending to lengthen and others to shorten the cylinder.

Let us go back to the real hat once more, with our newly acquired knowledge of illusions and

[1] One of the laws of illusion is that when two or more motives tend in the same direction the satisfying of one tends to satisfy the other in part. The total effect of the co-operating illusions mentioned is therefore not fully as large as is here represented.

their measurement. Let the reader set a silk hat on his head and invite some one to break off a broom straw so that it shall seem to the observer that when he holds the straw in a horizontal position, touching the hat with one end, it looks to be equal to the shorter diameter at the top of the crown; then let him take another straw in the same position and on it estimate the height of the hat at the longest point of the cylinder. If the observer is careful and does not know what to expect, his measurements will correspond well with the above theoretical constructions; that is, the diameter of the hat will be overestimated by about twelve per cent. and the height by about thirty per cent.

But the visitor may ask for an explanation. Different theories have been advanced to explain the illusion of the vertical. According to the commonly accepted theory, it is due to the fact that linear distances are judged in terms of eye movement, and those muscles which move the eyes in a horizontal plane are large and much used, while those which move them in the vertical plane are smaller and less used. These facts lead to the overestimation of the vertical movement of the eyeball, and hence to overestimation of the vertical distance. The three new illusions are all proved by experiment to be so-called "association" illusions; that is, there are some irrelevant ideas in the background of consciousness at the time of perception, and these ideas, or vague feelings, unconsciously "flow" into the percept. In the case of the area-illusion it is a vague feeling of "more of it" with reference to the area as compared with the line; and, in the case of the volume-illusion, it is a vague notion of "more of it" with reference to the surface of the solid as compared with a mere surface, which leads to the overestimation. It does so because the discriminating consciousness is not keen enough to segregate these irrelevant factors from the space judgment. In like manner, the cylinder suggests length—a sort of reaching out—which the diameter does not suggest, and this deeply ingrained craving for length, not being checked, expresses itself in the actual perception of the additional length. Space does not permit a detailed account of these explanations.

These four facts concerning errors in the perception of the hat may be stated as laws of illusion. Thus we say that vertical distances, as compared with horizontal distances, are overestimated. Surfaces, as compared with lines, are overestimated. Linear dimensions on surfaces of objects having volume, as compared with mere lines, or with surfaces, are overestimated. The length of a

LAW IN ILLUSION

cylinder, as compared with its diameter, or with areal or linear distance, is overestimated. These are laws of illusion, and are quite as real as what we ordinarily call laws in other phases of nature. The fact that they may have exceptions but helps to prove the rule. A great many laws are known for each of these and related illusions. It would be easy in our present knowledge to state many laws of each of these illusions, but we conclude with this stage of the analysis.

The most significant thing in regard to such a study is that having the elaboration and explanation of an illusion in one situation makes possible its application in analogous cases. Here are some cases in point which may be readily confirmed by the reader:

Ask some one to estimate the depth of a teacup by marking on the bowl end of a teaspoon how high the top of the cup will reach when the teaspoon is set upright in the cup. A good observer (who is without knowledge of the nature and force of the illusion) will mark a place fully twenty-five per cent. too high on the spoon.

Ask some one to estimate the height of a flour barrel in terms of its greatest diameter. There will be an overestimation of nearly twenty per cent.

Stand with arms outstretched so as to form a

cross with the body, and ask a person to judge the relative length of measure from finger-tip to finger-tip in terms of the height. Calling the height ten units, how many units are there in the reach? The reach may be underestimated by more than twenty per cent.

Before leaving this illustration let me impress once more the fact of the common occurrence of these illusions. All vertical distances, all linear distances or areas, all surfaces on voluminous objects, the length of all cylinders—all tend to be overestimated regardless of form or regularity, regardless of whether the object is natural, artificial, or merely a geometric line. These illusions are all in the house as well as in the hat; they are all in the bird as well as in the cup; they are all in the picture of a man as well as in the line or drawing of the cylinder (No. 15, Fig. 19). Knowing their causes, we can trace them in every setting.[1]

If one is impressed with the futility of knowing all laws of illusion, he must at the same time be impressed, from observations like these, with the extraordinarily wide application we may make of the knowledge of a few leading principles of illusion.

[1] What seems to be an exception to the rule is merely the canceling of one motive for illusion by another opposing motive, as, for example, in the experiment with the cylinder in the horizontal position.

LAW IN ILLUSION

There are relationships between silk hats, flour barrels, teacups, standpipes, the human body, and a block of ice cream. Psychologically we soon form the habit of seeing objects in terms of elements, such as lines. surfaces, and solids of various types. In the case under consideration, objects represented in Fig. 19 were examined in turn and a list of the normal illusions was determined for each of these elemental types of form. With this array of qualitative and quantitative facts, partially reduced to habits of perception at command, the world takes on a different appearance as compared with our view of it before possession of this knowledge; there is very real satisfaction in being able to know the cause of the errors and how to make allowance for them.

THE MEDICINE BOTTLE: ILLUSIONS OF WEIGHT

Everyone is familiar with the old quibble or problem: Which is the heavier, a pound of lead or a pound of feathers? Probably none of those who asked that question in the distant past realized the nature of the principle that underlies the query. Before proceeding, the reader should perform, preferably upon some one else who does not know of the illusion, one of the following tests:

Place a down pillow on one hand and on the other a light tumbler into which water may be poured until the weight of the glass of water seems to be equal to the weight of the pillow.

Inflate a large empty paper bag and tie it up air tight. Place the bag on the palm of one hand and into the palm of the other hand take such a quantity of coin or other metal as will seem to equal the bag in weight.[1]

This is a startling situation. No one can fully realize the enormity of the illusion without really trying the experiment. After this actual experience of illusion in weight, we are prepared to trace the scope and ramifications of the general relation involved. For this purpose let us take a single intensive illustration of the operation of law in illusion in a case like this. Let us take the simple everyday act of lifting an opaque medicine bottle to tell by weight how much it contains.

In order to give some idea of the number of laws of illusion which may appear in a single, simple act like this, I shall first name ten well-known normal

[1] If the observer does not know of the illusion or suspect it, the paper bag will be found to weigh from ten to twenty times as much as the metal with which it was matched, and the pillow from three to ten times as much as the glass and the water it contained. The discrepancy would be proportionately larger if heavy metal were used in place of water.

illusions which may be involved here. Then, to show that for each of these illusions there are many specific laws, I shall name ten laws under one of these ten illusions. If space permitted, it would be quite possible in most cases to give ten separate laws for each of these ten illusions, for the laws of illusion which may apply in this common act are numerous.

In this one act of lifting a common object with the hand, the following ten are among the well-known illusions which have been proved in quantitative measurements:

Position.—The apparent weight of an object is most correctly judged when the object is lifted in the most natural and convenient position of the arm and hand. The reaching out of the hand in any direction leads to overestimation of the weight. This is known as the space-error. The bottle feels heavier when one reaches up on a shelf and first touches it than when the arm is in a natural position.

Grasp.—The same object seems to be heavier when grasped lightly than when grasped tightly. If the bottle which is reached for is supposed to be empty, but actually is more or less filled, its weight will be overestimated because it is grasped too lightly.

Area.—The object appears to be heavier if lifted in contact with a small area. The bottle seems lighter when it is grasped with the whole hand than when lifted with the finger-tips.

Rate.—The object seems heavier if lifted by a slow movement than if lifted by a quick, though not jerking, movement.

Holding.—A heavy weight grows heavier and a light weight grows lighter when sustained undisturbed in the hand. A penny placed in the palm of the hand will first be clearly felt, but after five minutes it will not be felt at all if the observer has held his hand perfectly still.

Sequence.—An object of moderate weight appears to be heavier or lighter than it really is according as a lighter or a heavier object has been lifted just previously. If a four-ounce bottle has been lifted just before a two-ounce bottle, the latter will be underestimated; whereas if a half-ounce bottle has been lifted just before the two-ounce bottle, the latter will be overestimated. This is due to the principle of contrast; if two equal weights are lifted in sequence, the second appears to be the heavier. This last statement is a familiar law of sensation and is known as the time-error.

Division of Energy.—An object held in one hand appears to be lighter than it really is if the other hand supports another weight or is otherwise engaged, as in a grasp or push. The bottle will seem lighter than if the hand were free, if one hangs by the other hand on the arm of a chair.

Temperature.—Any deviation from the physiological zero of temperature increases the apparent weight of an object. If the bottle is very warm or very cold it will seem heavy. It is easy to double the apparent weight of a silver dollar by merely changing its temperature.

Material.—An object appears to be heavier or lighter than it really is according as the appearance of the material of which it is made suggests a heavier or a lighter weight than the actual. If the contents of the bottle could be dimly seen and seemed to suggest mercury, although it were really an oil, the weight would be greatly underestimated; whereas if it seemed to be empty, but were filled with oil, its weight would be quite as strongly overestimated.

Size-weight.—Any deviation from a central, neutral relation of size to weight in an object leads to illusion. If the size of the object is relatively large, its weight will be underestimated; if relatively small, it will be overestimated. Of two objects that are of the same weight, but differing in size, the larger appears to be the lighter when lifted.[1]

Let us now take the last mentioned of these illusions, which is the one most directly suggested by the experiments with the pillow and the paper bag, and view it in some detail as it may enter into the lifting of the medicine bottle. For all normal individuals there is in every type of object a given weight which we may call neutral, for which there is no size-weight illusion; all objects like it, but differing in size, are subject to the illusion. In general, objects which are smaller will be overestimated in weight, and objects which are larger will be underestimated. Thus all bouquets are underestimated, and all solid pieces of jewelry are overestimated in weight. Roughly we may classify on the one side relatively light objects, such as feathers, paper, flowers, empty bags, clothes, and hay;

---

[1] It would be quite logical to subsume several of these illusions under one generic class which we might call the Specific Gravity weight-illusion, and formulate it something like this: If the specific gravity of an object is lower than the central, neutral specific gravity, the weight of that object will be underestimated; whereas if the specific gravity of an object is higher than the neutral specific gravity, the weight of the object will be overestimated. This rule clearly includes the ninth and tenth above, and indirectly it includes the second, third, fourth, and fifth, as the forces there involved are secondary resultants of the specific gravity impression.

and, on the other, relatively heavy objects, such as mercury, solid metals, stone, and perhaps water. Although there are numerous conditions which must be taken into account, and it is by no means a fixed ratio, we may have a rough knowledge of what ordinarily represents a practically neutral size-weight, or specific gravity, by remembering that, ordinarily, a solid piece of oak wood comes near being neutral. Books are not far from neutral, though usually heavier;[1] letters and clothing are probably lighter. Or, to give a general intimation of the force of the illusion in common objects: if one bottle is seven times the volume of another, but is equal to it in weight and like it except in size, the smaller will seem to be about twice as heavy as the larger. If a ball weighs as much as a "Derby" hat, the ball will seem to weigh about twice as much as the hat. If a man is asked to match the weight of his golf cap with coins, it will be found that the cap actually weighs three or four times as much as the coins laid out in the estimate. Such comparisons as these may be tested in actual experiment by anyone interested.

This brief survey should convey two facts: first, that illusions of this kind occur for all normal per-

[1] Dry oak weighs about .65 gr. to the c. c.; books, .81 gr.; and water, 1 gr.

sons; and, second, that they are predictable as to direction and approximate amount.

But how can such facts be determined? How can the illusions be measured? To illustrate in the case of the medicine bottle, we may take as a standard, or neutral basis, a wooden bottle 42 mm. in diameter and 42 mm. in height, filled with water so as to weigh 50 gr., which is about the weight of a solid oak cylinder of the same size. We may then take another bottle of any size and, by varying the amount of its contents, find how heavy it must be to match the standard bottle in apparent weight. All measurements for bottles of different sizes which are made in terms of the same standard are, of course, comparable. Thus, in order to seem equal to the standard in weight, a bottle twice as large as the standard must weigh about 58 gr., while a bottle half as large as the standard need weigh only about 37 gr. to seem equal to the 50-gr. standard.

In this way different illusions based on the relation of weight to size may be determined, and we may answer questions such as these: How does the illusion vary with size-weight relations? Under what conditions (if any) may it be eliminated? Is it normal? Is it negative or positive? What is its cause? How does it vary with the prominence of spatial imagery? How does it vary with intelligence, age, and sex? What use can be made of it? These questions I shall answer briefly in turn by stating in the form of laws some of the demonstrated facts of this size-weight illusion.

Size-weight.—This illusion varies in a geometric ratio with the object's deviation from that proportion of size to weight which in the same material would lead to a correct visual estimate of weight, and is known as neutral. For given conditions this law of variation in weight with variation in size has been determined in full detail. It may be expressed in equations or curves which make it possible to compute the amount of illusion for a given individual in any given size of a lifted object of a specific kind, as soon as the coefficient of illusion in a single measurement upon this individual for this kind of object is known.

Persistence.—(1) This illusion remains undiminished and tends to grow more constant with long-continued practice so long as the observer is not aware of its existence. This remarkable law was first determined by selecting four of the keenest observers available, who did not know of the illusion, and giving them each twenty consecutive days (one hour a day) of the most effective training that could be devised.[1] The results for the four observers agreed entirely in showing no improvement with this training, and thus established the above law.

(2) The force of the illusion is decreased when its existence becomes known or suspected. When the four observers above mentioned had finished their training without knowledge, the illusion was thoroughly explained to them and another measurement was taken. Under these conditions the illusion was diminished to practically one-half of its original force.

(3) The motive for the illusion can perhaps never be eradicated by practice. The illusion persists permanently in spite of continued practice and knowledge about it. Persons who have been experimenting with this illusion for the last twenty years are still subject to it in spite of the fact that they have exact knowledge of its nature and conditions.

[1] To show that the men chosen were intelligent, the career of one of them is *apropos*: He entered Yale in the senior year practically penniless. During that year he took honors in oratory, debate, and athletics, and earned his expenses. He then gained the degree of Doctor of Philosophy and that of Doctor of Civil Law in course, in the minimum time, and by the end of that time he had laid up enough money to marry and spend his honeymoon abroad. He was a keen fellow, yet he differed from the other observers only in that his illusion was more constant.

(4) One soon learns to make conscious allowance for it. Although, to the long-trained observer, the pound of lead and the pound of feathers never seem equal, he is not deceived by the illusion because, after varied measurements, he knows just what allowance to make for it.

(5) There is a general tendency to make allowance for it unconsciously. This often results in an overcorrection, sometimes very decided, although the observer may not be conscious of having made any correction.

Normal.—The size-weight illusion is a normal illusion. By this we mean that its motives are present in all normal persons under normal conditions for perception of weight.[1] Instead of being a sign of weakness, its normal force is a sign of mental keenness.

---

[1] In demonstrating a similar illusion in sight to a class one day, the lecturer said: "You observe that this line, which is actually straight, looks bent." All the class, except one young man, verified the observation. He said, "It looks straight to me." Then, presenting the complementary phase of the illusion, the lecturer said: "You observe that this line, which is actually bent, looks straight." All agreed except the same young man. He said, "That line looks bent to me." The lecturer thereupon made closer observation and found that the young man was drunk, and reported him to the president, with the result that the wretch was expelled from the university within two hours from the time that he had proved refractory to a normal illusion. Moral!

PSYCHOLOGY IN DAILY LIFE

Negative.—The size-weight illusion is negative. In this respect it is contrasted with the positive illusion. In the positive illusion we perceive what we expect to perceive; in the negative, we perceive in a certain sense the opposite of what we expect. In taking up two bottles, a large one and a small one, but both of about the same weight, we approach the larger with a semi-conscious feeling that it ought to be heavier, but we find it very distinctly lighter than the other.

Preadjustment.—Before lifting an object we always make a muscular preadjustment upon a preliminary estimate of weight, usually through sight. If the weight of the lifted object corresponds to this preadjustment, there will be no illusion, and the object may be said to be neutral. But if the object is too heavy for this preadjustment its weight will be overestimated; whereas, if it is too light for the preadjustment, its weight will be underestimated. Herein is the key to the explanation of this illusion.

In general, we put forth more energy for the lifting of a large object than for a small one. There are so few discrepancies between size and weight that the practice has become an automatic and deeply ingrained habit, which proves to be an essential condition for efficient lifting. The fact that this habit is at work when we are lifting may be observed in introspection; but we also find objective evidence to show that, when lifting a large bottle and a small bottle, both of which contain the same amount of liquid, the larger is grasped more tightly and the smaller one tends to slip through the fingers. We lift the larger both faster and higher than the smaller bottle. These observations are direct evidence of the difference in preadjustment for the two bottles. The fact that this habitual tendency to gravitate toward the central adjustment depending upon size, in the face of practice, knowledge, sense-impression, or reason (as in the persistence of the illusion after we know the actual weight of the pillow and the lead or the actual weight of the two bottles), is a beautiful proof of the fixity in the organization of the interpretative aspect of our normal perception.

Spatial Sense.—The illusion varies with the prominence of the spatial percept or image. This has been demonstrated in several ways. In the original experiment on this point, four series of measurements were made with a series of cylinders varying in diameter only, under the following conditions: (1) The cylinders were seen directly in the lifting, as is ordinarily done. (2) They were lifted by handles attached by short silk threads so that when the observer looked at the handle in the hand he would see the cylinder in indirect vision. (3) The cylinders to be lifted were seen for a moment and then the observer with closed eyes lifted them by the handles. (4) The weights were again lifted by the handles, but the observer was blindfolded and kept entirely ignorant of the size of the object which he was lifting.

The results show very clearly (1) that the illusion is strongest when the observer sees the weight directly while lifting; (2) that it is weaker when the observer sees the weight only in indirect vision while lifting; (3) that it is still weaker when the observer has only a memory image of the size of the weight, and (4) that, when the size of the weight is unknown, there is no trace of the illusion.

With seeing persons the illusion is caused by the visual impression for the preadjustment. It was therefore thought worth while to determine whether the blind were subject to the illusion. Measurements made upon the blind proved that the illusion is of the same force and of the same degree of constancy for them as for seeing persons. In their case touch takes the place of sight for the preadjustment.

In another series of experiments with seeing persons the observers were blindfolded and allowed to learn the size of the object only through touch and the muscle sense, and it was shown that the illusion is stronger under this condition than when based on sight, probably because the difficulty in the perception of size makes the observer more conscious of size.

Intelligence.—The illusion is of medium degree and most constant in force for the most reliable observers. A poor observer may show a very large or a very small illusion, as the chance may be; but the average tends to be about the same as for a good observer. This law, like the law of persistence, was a surprise to the first investigators, as it had always been assumed that subjection to such an illusion was characteristic of a poor observer. Now we know that normality in this illusion is a sign of sensory keenness.[1] The law has been verified in several ways. The force of the illusion has been correlated with mental brightness of school children as estimated by teachers, as judged from school records, and as measured in special tests of bright-

---

[1] In discussing intelligence in this connection, it is necessary to bear in mind that a person may be a logical prodigy or a memory prodigy without being keen in sense observation. A brilliant student in history or language may have a very poor capacity for judging weight or other measures. Brightness in the present sense should therefore mean keenness in sense observation.

ness. It has been correlated with measures of sensory discrimination for weight and other senses; in all these cases the above law has been sustained. The most striking proof, however, comes from an examination of the children in a school for the retarded. It was found that feeble-minded children who are greatly retarded in mental development are not subject to the illusion.

Age.—The illusion is stronger for children than for adults. This has been interpreted to mean that children do not have the same mental capacity as the adult; and hence the illusion. But a careful analysis of the fact leads us to the conclusion that the difference is not in the mental capacity but rather in the possession of information. We know that the illusion decreases greatly with knowledge, and, since the opportunity for knowing about an illusion is at the present time comparatively very much greater for an adult than for a child, it seems fair to account for the difference largely on the score of difference in information rather than in terms of mental development, particularly as the illusion does not vary with intelligence in normal individuals.

Sex.—The illusion is stronger for women than for men. This is a constant and very striking feature. It is one of the clearest cases in point to prove that, in the field of sensory discrimination, woman is more susceptible than man. It is not a question of intelligence, though it may be in part a question of information; but it rather points to an important anthropological fact in sex difference of which this illusion offers a fine opportunity for investigation. Young boys and girls do not differ in this respect.

Use.—Among others, the following four laws for the practical use of the illusion have been demonstrated:

(1) By employing this illusion it is possible to increase the maximum lifting power. If we take an empty flour barrel and a half-peck measure and attach the same kind of handle to each, and load the half-peck measure with lead to such an extent that a given observer can just hold it for ten seconds on the straight arm; and if we then put the half-peck measure with its load into the barrel and ask the observer to lift the barrel containing the half-peck measure with its maximum weight and the handle, all together, he will be able to hold the barrel and all its contents for ten seconds.

(2) By employing the illusion a person may be able to perform a given amount of physical labor with less fatigue than without the illusion. A pump handle may be so constructed as to illustrate this

use; it need only be made comparatively large and light.

(3) By employing this illusion, sensory discrimination may be made more efficient. If a good observer be asked to detect a very small difference between two eight-ounce bottles, each containing an ounce of mercury, he will probably be able to detect a difference of one-fifteenth of the actual weight, whereas if the same amount of mercury be put into half-ounce bottles, he will be likely to detect a difference as small as one-thirtieth of the actual weight.

(4) By making a correction for this illusion the conformity of one of the fundamental laws of sensation, Weber's law of the relativity of sense differences, will be increased. It is now recognized that, if this illusion is involved in measurements on Weber's law, a coefficient of correction for the illusion must be introduced.

THINGS ARE NOT WHAT THEY SEEM, BUT THERE IS METHOD IN OUR ERRORS

After laboring through this maze of illusions, we are prepared to ask and answer the question: What is a normal illusion? We may say a normal illusion is a normal, predictable error of sense. The term illusion is used interchangeably, sometimes to designate the amount of error and at other times to designate the total erroneous perception. Thus, if one consistently sees a 100-mm. line as only 75 mm. long, we may speak of the extent of the illusion as equivalent to twenty-five per cent., or we may speak of the seventy-five per cent. actually perceived as the illusion; the context, however, always makes clear which one of these meanings is used. The condition that causes the illusion we have called its motive.

The aim in this chapter has been threefold: first, to show that motives for normal illusion are ever present in the ordinary use of our senses; second, that there is law and orderliness in every phase of these illusions; and, third, that it is not only a pleasure and a deep source of satisfaction but also a matter of decidedly practical importance to know the laws of behavior in these illusions.

If it be borne in mind that the discussion of these three concrete cases has brought us into touch with hundreds of illusions, and that what is true of these simple sensory experiences is probably equally true of our vast life of sensory experiences as a whole, we realize in a very startling way that things are not what they seem. Color, form, direction, brightness, and distance, in sight; pitch, duration, intensity, localization, and harmony, in hearing; and so on, through all of the senses—every attribute of every sensation is subject to illusion.

Normal illusions are like microbes; they are ever present, and they may be beneficent or noxious, but without them life as it now is could not exist. Since the discovery of microbes and the discovery of normal illusions, a man who holds himself free from illusions is like the schoolhouse janitor who indignantly resented the insinuation that there had been microbes in the schoolhouse since he had taken charge of it. He had not seen a single microbe.

Abnormal illusions are comparatively rare, but there is law in these quite as certainly as in normal illusion.

The first impression of the student of psychology of illusion is one of confusion. That which he had trusted and by which he had guided himself is questioned, proved unreliable, and often wrong. But this realization of a tearing-down process is necessary in order that he may become interested in securing a genuine insight into the true nature of things. As he proceeds in the subject he naturally classifies sources of error, sees relationships, acquires serviceable guiding principles, and finds greater and greater satisfaction in seeing how and why events occur in his mental life.

LAW IN ILLUSION

Is there, then, law in illusion? To many the constant use of the term law in a field so flimsy and flitting as that of illusion may seem loose and extravagant. Law is in general used to designate an established, predictable mode of behavior; that is just the behavior of mental life which we have attempted to illustrate. Those who have not studied science often have a false notion to the effect that law is rigid, not subject to fluctuation, and complete. In ninety-nine cases out of a hundred these three assumptions are false. Take for example the laws of growth of the human body—never exact, always variable, and never completely known in all their ramifications; yet these are accepted as laws. It is exactly in the same sense that the term law as applied to illusion is used in this chapter.

Current scientific theory postulates law and orderliness of nature whether it be physical or mental; and as soon as we begin to search in mental nature, be it the most fixed or the most apparently chaotic, we find, at every turn, law and order. One of the charms of the study of illusions is the progressive realization of insight into the orderliness, even a consummate complex of orderliness, in mental life.

CHAPTER VII

MENTAL MEASUREMENT

In order to illustrate the scope and significance of mental measurement in a concrete and specific instance, I shall venture to present a psychological outline of the measurement of an individual as a singer. Let us assume that this individual is a girl, fifteen years of age, who has had musical training and now desires the best obtainable advice from a consulting psychologist in music in regard to her future prospects as a singer.

OUTLINE OF MEASUREMENTS ON AN INDIVIDUAL AS A SINGER

Musical power is generally admitted to embrace certain well-recognized and fairly concrete capacities. In our commonplace judgments about ourselves and others we say: "I have no ear for music," "I cannot tell a chord from a discord," "I cannot keep time," "I have no sense of rhythm," "I cannot tell a two-step from a waltz," "I cannot

196

remember tunes," "I cannot image sounds," "I am not moved by music," "I do not enjoy music." Or, if speaking of some one who has musical ability, we say: "He has a deep, rich voice," "he never forgets an air," "he lives in song." Such judgments have reference to generally admitted specific factors involved in musical capacity by virtue of a "musical" organization. Corresponding to these judgments of native capacity we have judgments about musical education, about musical environment, about special influences and stimuli for the development of musical talent, and about technique and success in the rendition of music. When such judgments are based upon measurements, classified, and adequately interpreted, they may constitute a measure of the individual as a singer.

This measure should consist of a number of representative measurements upon specific capacities and achievements, and these should be supplemented by a full survey through systematic observation and by other verified information bearing upon the valuation of the individual as a singer.

If we classify the measurements on the basis of the characteristics of tones, we shall have three classes dealing respectively with pitch, intensity (loudness), and time. On the other hand, if we classify them on the basis of the mental processes involved in the appreciation and expression of music, we may arrange them into four groups, namely, sensory, motor, associational, and affective. In the following list of measurements these two classifications are so combined as to yield a comprehensive survey.

LIST OF MEASUREMENTS ON A SINGER

I. Sensory (ability to hear music).
    A. Pitch.
        1. Discrimination ("musical ear").
        2. Survey of register.
        3. Tonal range: (a) upper limit, (b) lower limit.
        4. Timbre (tone color).
        5. Consonance and dissonance (harmony).
    B. Intensity (loudness).
        1. Sensibility (hearing-ability).
        2. Discrimination (capacity for intellectual use).
    C. Time.
        1. Sense of time (duration and intensity).
        2. Sense of rhythm.

II. Motor (ability to sing).
    A. Pitch.
        1. Striking a tone.
        2. Varying a tone.

      3. Singing intervals.
      4. Sustaining a tone.
      5. Registers.
      6. Timbre: (a) purity, (b) richness, (c) mellowness, (d) clearness, (e) flexibility.
      7. Plasticity: curves of learning.

  B. Intensity.
      1. Natural strength and volume of voice.
      2. Voluntary control.
      3. Rhythmic expression.

  C. Time.
      1. Motor ability.
      2. Transition and attack.
      3. Singing in time.

III. Associational (ability to imagine, remember and think in music).

  A. Imagery.
      1. Type.
      2. Rôle of auditory and motor images.

  B. Memory.
      1. Memory span.
      2. Retention.
      3. Redintegration.

  C. Ideation.
      1. Association type and musical content.
      2. Musical grasp.
      3. Creative imagination.
      4. Plasticity: curves of learning.

IV. Affective (ability to feel music).
    A. Likes and dislikes: character of musical appeal.
        1. Pitch, timbre, melody and harmony.
        2. Intensity and volume.
        3. Time and rhythm.
    B. Emotional reaction to music.
    C. Power of æsthetic interpretation in singing.

This is a list of technical measurements which may be made by instruments and methods now available in a psychological laboratory. They are so selected as to furnish an adequate survey of the individual through a relatively small number of records on representative capacities. The measuring of an individual in this way is called psychography, which means making a graphic record of mental capacity.

In a well-equipped psychological laboratory we have instruments by which all these measurements may be made with a considerable degree of accuracy. Among these instruments are series of tuning forks for the measurement of the hearing of pitch in its various changes and combinations, instruments for the measuring of ability in hearing of modifications of loudness in sound, instruments for measuring time-sense and the sense of rhythm, instruments recording the pitch, loudness, and time-features of tones in singing, and instruments for the control of observations of more complex processes. For our present purpose it is not necessary to describe, or even to name them. It is, however, necessary at this stage that we shall have a general notion of what the listed measurements represent. For this we need not appeal to technical knowledge of either music or psychology, but may couch our conception in terms of our common knowledge of matters musical and psychological.

The object of sensory measurement is to determine to what extent the individual is psycho-physically capable of hearing music. What is generally known as "musical ear" is measured in terms of the ability to hear small differences in the pitch of two successive tones. This is called "pitch discrimination." One person may be able to hear a difference of one-hundredth of a tone, while another may not be able to hear a difference of a half-tone. This record is usually taken at a', the first a above middle c, which is in the middle register of the ear. But the keenness of the ear varies for different parts of the register. It is therefore necessary to make a survey of the relative keenness of the ear at a few representative points between the upper and the lower limits of pitch. The tonal range of the ear is measured by determining respectively the highest and the lowest tone that can be heard. One person may be able to hear tones as high as 40,000 vibrations per second, while another may not be able to hear a tone only half as high. The timbre of a tone is what is ordinarily spoken of as quality or tone-color. The keenness of the ear for the perception of timbre may be measured by determining the ability to distinguish small differences in timbre. The sense of harmony may be measured by determining the ability of the individual in the arranging of a number of series of pairs of tones in the order of their consonance. In all these tests we must distinguish between native capacity and skill acquired through training. At this stage we are interested in the former only.

For the attribute of intensity, we should have at least two sensory measures: (1) the hearing-ability of each ear for tones, and (2) the ability to hear variations in the strength of a familiar, relatively pure, musical tone. These measures will show the natural capacity of the individual for the hearing of faint tones, the hearing of intensity accent, and the hearing of shadings in the strength and volume of tones in musical expression. The perception of volume is so intimately dependent upon the perception of strength of tone, that a separate measure is not needed.

Rhythm may be expressed through both time and intensity. For a single measurement of the perception of rhythm as a time element, we may eliminate intensity and measure the least perceptible deviation in the duration of the recurrent sound, uniform in all respects except duration.

There are four fundamental phases of simple pitch singing which should be examined separately: (1) ability to reproduce the pitch of a tone heard one second before the singing; (2) ability to make faint shadings (sharp and flat) in pitch; (3) ability to sing intervals, and (4) ability to sustain a tone, both with reference to periodic and progressive changes in pitch. The record of the ability to strike the pitch of the tone should be taken at the middle, and at points near the upper and the lower limits of the musical register of the voice. The voluntary control of the pitch of the voice, or ability in the varying of a tone, is measured in terms of the minimal producible sharp or flat. The measure of ability in singing intervals should be taken for the singing of both the natural scale and the chromatic scale. The ability to sustain the pitch of a tone evenly for ten seconds may also be measured at the three representative levels of the register, and should be so recorded as to show both progressive and periodic changes. Progressive changes are tendencies to gradually sharp or flat; periodic changes may be either regular fluctuations in pitch, or a general lack of control.

The register of the voice should be stated in terms of the characteristic changes in timbre which take place near the upper and lower limits. Thus we may determine the range for agreeable musical tones, for tones easily sung, for chest tones, and for true pitch singing. This series of records should be supplemented by a systematic description of the progressive change in the character of the tone from one end of the register to the other.

Under the head of timbre of the voice, the psychological-æsthetic effect we seek to measure is the degree of beauty of the objective tone. We therefore eliminate subjective and circumstantial conditions and accessory features of the singer which may modify the agreeableness and disagreeableness of the given tone and consider beauty only as it is objective in the physical tone. This may be measured with considerable precision in terms of the form of the sound wave. From a single well-chosen graphic record of the voice, we may determine the following factors: (a) purity, the degree of approach to the smooth sine curve in the form of the wave; (b) richness, the number of overtones present; (c) mellowness, the character of the distribution of the overtones; (d) clearness, the uniformity in the form of a series of waves; (e) flexibility, the character of the progressive transition from one wave form to another. These purely objective measures of the beauty of the tone must be supplemented by systematic observations on the agreeableness of the timbre of the voice by experts judging separately each of the specific qualitative aspects of the voice as naturally used in singing. Objective record must also be made of the mode of tone production, especially of the characteristics of the resonance.

The plasticity of the individual in a given capacity is measured by the rate and character of the learning processes in that capacity. We now know enough of the characteristics of "learning curves" to be able to determine, in a relatively small number of trials, the character of the prospect that an individual may have for acquiring skill in any given activity. The plasticity may be measured in this way for any of the motor processes of musical training. If but a single measure of plasticity is to be made, this may well be on the training in accuracy of transition from one note to another, involving the elements of release and attack of tones.

As regards intensity in tone production, we are interested in the natural strength and volume of the tone and in the voluntary control of these factors. The strength of tone is expressed in terms of amplitude of vibration and may be measured in representative parts of the register. Carrying power and volume, in so far as they differ from strength, may be judged essentially in terms of the mode of tone production.

Motor ability may be measured in terms of the degree of accuracy in the rapid enunciation of a selected list of syllables. The form of the attack is also an excellent measure of time-efficiency in musical action. But the most important of all time measurements is of course the ability to sing in accurate time and rhythm. For time alone, we test by singing equal durations without accent; for rhythm, in the true sense, the singing must be done with time and intensity-variables together as in ordinary singing.

A number of tests may be grouped under the general head of Association, and these may be subdivided somewhat arbitrarily as in the outlined classification. We should first secure a quantitative picture of the relative vividness of images from the different senses. Then the auditory image should be tested for fidelity, stability, and relevance, in such a way as to reflect the rôle and power of auditory imagery in singing. The same may also be done for motor imagery.

The most fundamental fact about memory is its span for musical tones. This may be measured in terms of the number of tones (taken from a single octave, but not forming a known melody) the individual can remember for immediate reproduction or recognition. The power of retention may be measured by determining roughly the extent to which the singer can recall music heard a day or a week before. The power of musical redintegration may be tested by observing to what extent the individual can recall in their true setting the fine details of a complex musical production.

Free association experiments as employed in what is now called psychoanalysis may be so arranged as to determine the characteristic "musical content" and the prevailing mode of reaction to music. The mental content is different in the natural appreciation of the ragtime, the hymn, and the grand opera; one mind is naturally equipped for the appreciation of one kind of music, another mind for another type.

To the musical mind sounds group themselves in large units, such as themes, movements, phrases. The power of grasp for musical complexes may be measured in terms of a graded series of complexes of musical units, taking in turn the various factors of pitch (including timbre, melody, and harmony), intensity, and time.

A record of creative imagination may be obtained under experimental conditions by allowing the singer to improvise a tune for a selected stanza. The words of a series of stanzas should convey different types of emotional value. Here the greatest freedom should be allowed the singer for spontaneous expression. The ability manifested in such a production may then be measured in terms of the merit of such a composition as preserved in the dictograph.

As knowledge of ability in learning music is essential, the mode of forming and the natural ability for acquiring new musical associations should be measured for one or more phases of vocal training, such as the placing of the voice, singing the chromatic intervals, or the analysis of clangs. If a single representative measure were to be made this might profitably be the establishment of the learning curve for the singing of intervals.

The affective phase of music is never isolated from the cognitive and motor elements, for both of these always involve some feeling. In such measurements as those of consonance, association type, and creative imagination, we deal with facts which are quite as relevant to the affective as to the cognitive side of consciousness. The same principle applies also to some of the motor examples. The musical emotions are conditioned upon the various powers of appreciation and expression which we have just reviewed. Unless our singer has capacity for hearing or expressing a given musical effect, she cannot experience emotional pleasure in it. The sensory, motor, and associational measurements have therefore determined in part the presence or absence of capacity for affective or emotional appreciation and expression. There are, however, three general surveys which are of a positive and fundamental nature; namely, musical preferences, reaction to musical effects, and power of interpretation in singing.

One affective aspect of the character of the musical appreciation may be measured by determining the curve of likes and dislikes for representative series of musical selections. These should be so arranged as to represent the main types of musical appeal through each of the attributes of sound. Here the measurement may be standardized by having the graded selections furnished in a series of the best quality of phonograph discs. Three series might be used: (1) the pitch, timbre, and harmony series; (2) the intensity and volume series; and (3) the time or rhythm series.

The amount and character of reaction to different musical effects may be observed under experimental conditions when the observer is not aware that this is being done. Thus a systematic record of such observations may be made under the guise of repeating the preceding measurement (IV, A, 1) in which the observer works by the method of impression just outlined. The curve for different kinds of mental and physical reactions observed may be made to parallel and supplement the curves for agreeableness and disagreeableness.

There are two aspects to the power of interpretation of music in singing, namely, its appreciation and its expression. Since expression involves appreciation, measurement on appreciation may be omitted. The power of expression may be measured by methods now in vogue for the measuring of merit. Musical experts may be obtained to make comparisons of one specific element in singing after another under experimental conditions.

As a supplement to these measurements, there must be other measurements, statistical data, biographical information, and free observations regarding musical training, traits of temperament and attitude, spontaneous tendencies in the pursuit of music, general education and non-musical accomplishments, social circumstances, and physique.

INTERPRETATION OF THESE MEASUREMENTS

With this tentative plan of procedure before us as a concrete instance to consider, let us ask and answer the following three questions: How do these measurements acquire unity and meaning? Do they constitute an adequate measure of the singer? Of what practical significance can they be?

With reference to the first of these questions, it is apparent that such a group of measurements is merely a group of samples of measurements. Their unity and meaning depend upon the degree to which they are adequately representative, and are interpreted in true perspective.

They have meaning only when compared with previously established norms, which show the mode and extent of distribution for a sufficiently large number of cases, and when interpreted in the light of the meaning ascribed to each level in the distribution. Take, for illustration, discriminative action in voluntary control of the pitch of the voice in singing. Reference to our norms shows, for example, that a record of .9 vibration means that this ability is within 3 per cent. of the best record for individuals under similar conditions, and that those who have such control are thoroughly qualified to render difficult music accurately in this respect; while a record of 9 vibrations falls within 8 per cent. of the poorest ability measured, and is characteristic of an individual who cannot sing; whereas a record of 3 vibrations represents the average ability of an untrained individual.

These norms must be determined with much labor and skill in the interest of an avowedly applied psychology, and must be undertaken as independent problems before yielding measurements of practical service. During the last few years a group of research students in the laboratory under my direction have been engaged in determining eight such norms in the psychology of music. After extensive preliminary development of methods and measuring instruments, they have aimed to secure records on two hundred individuals, constituting a homogeneous group for each norm. These norms are: pitch discrimination, vividness of tone imagery, span of tone-memory, consonance and dissonance, rhythmic action, intensity-discrimination, voluntary control of the pitch of the voice, and the singing of intervals. This is no simple undertaking, and the work must be regarded as preliminary. It requires the development of a technical method for each case, and the measurement must be made under as many conditions as it is desired to vary under control.

It is not possible to reduce the technical methods to a mechanical form so that every music teacher can use it. Even after means and methods have been invented and standardized and norms have been established, the measurement requires an expert, trained in the technique and skilled in the art—a consulting psychologist in music who devotes himself to it professionally. He must be able not only to determine the relative rank of a record by reference to the normal chart, but he must also be able to interpret the meaning of this rank in the light of the construction which has been placed upon the norm. He must be not only a technician, but an artist with appreciation for music, resourceful, sympathetic, and incisive in his interpretation. Like the so-called mind reader, he must have at his command a large repertory of procedures and be skilled in gathering information from all sorts of expected and unexpected sources during the experimental control. In this art he progressively simplifies the procedure, divests himself of mechanical contrivances wherever possible, and directs the singer under more and more natural conditions.

The expert in mental measurement always considers the human individual as a psycho-physical organism. He must have records for the physical as well as the mental endowments, and especially for their relationships; he must interpret each fact, physical or mental, as a feature of an organism, bearing in mind that there is organization in the mental just as truly as in the physical realm. With a clear grasp, on the one hand, of the fundamental attributes of objective music, and, on the other hand, of the fundamental capacities of the human organism for appreciating and rendering music, he must select the group of measurements suitable for his purpose. It may be a problem of learning; it may be an attempt to trace the nature of a discovered fault; it may be the measuring of progress made under a given mode of training. Our present schedule of measurements is a preliminary relief map. The measurements become effective and unified in so far as they are directed to one purpose.

Systematic observation and description are to be supplemented by concrete objective measurements. One of the main purposes of measurement is to secure experimental control of conditions in which systematic observation of factors under control may be recorded, though these do not enter into the numerical record.

The expert does not neglect what is available to

"common sense," as is often charged; he begins with this at its best, gradually culls and sifts his facts in systematic observation, and finally reaches a few of the representative features in objective measurements. The charge that the so-called "practical man" knows more through direct impression, or common sense, than the expert can discover scientifically is a flagrant expression of ignorance. The effect of the scientific point of view is not to belittle the significance of music or of man. But, on the contrary, as the astronomer sees more in the starry heavens than does the average man on a moonlight stroll, so the expert in the psychology of music beholds in music and in the human individual vastly more than the mere musician observes; for his vision is closer, more detailed, more keenly discriminating, recordable, repeatable, and more penetrating.

In the "Gibson" girl we see a realistic representation of form, face, hand, heart, and mind. No stroke has meaning by itself alone; no feature is really drawn; no mental faculty is actually represented in the cold, black lines. Yet, by a few rough strokes, the draughtsman has rendered an *ensemble* that adequately portrays the desired type of beauty in the expression of physical and mental life. One similarly conversant with mental measurements will bring together facts, that in themselves may seem meaningless, into an *ensemble* which, for our purpose, adequately represents the individual singer, or some feature of her capacity.

Turning to the second question, as to whether such a measure can be said in any sense to be adequate, let us take an illustration. A man has a richly varied and well cultivated garden. He is an horticulturist and cultivates the garden for scientific observation, pleasure, and service to his table. What would constitute an adequate measure of the garden? It is possible to determine to a high degree of accuracy the exact size, form, and weight of every living plant, the rate of growth of each and every leaf, root, flower, and fruit, the absorption rate for every chemical element drawn from the soil, the rate of increase in tensile strength, the deposit of chlorophyl, the internal structure of every cell, etc., *ad infinitum*. The possibility of measurement is here practically unlimited. An adequate measure is, however, not a complete measure, but one which answers a purpose. The gardener measures only the specific thing which he desires to know.

Now the human psycho-physical organism is at least as rich and as varied as a well-cultivated garden, if we may make so crude a comparison. While

MENTAL MEASUREMENT

mental measurements are not developed to the same degree of precision as are those of the gardener, they are, nevertheless, possible and may be quite as serviceable. The question is not how many measures are possible. No sane individual would ever undertake to make all possible measurements on a singer. The question is this: Can we command measurements which shall answer our present purpose? In the present case, do these measurements give us an adequate estimate of the various capacities and qualifications of this individual as a singer? The list here given is therefore not an attempt to show how many can be made, but to suggest which of those that are available may answer our purpose and, when taken together, prove an adequate measure.

Any desired mental measurement may be obtained, provided that we are willing to deal with specific facts. Our present list makes a formidable array, yet it is limited to those measurements for which the author knows methods and means of measurement, and to such as are essential to a reasonably representative survey of the matters to which they pertain. To the extent that they are representative and omit no essential feature, they constitute an adequate measure of an individual as a singer.

PSYCHOLOGY IN DAILY LIFE

It is not easy to reconcile the interests of psychology as a science with the demands in practical life for a single general measure for some practical purpose. Much work has been done on the naïve assumption that a single measure of a cognitive capacity should serve as a general measure of intelligence. Space discrimination, reaction after choice, the memory span, and other such specific cognitive measures have been used in seeking correlations with some sort of generally recognized "intelligence," but, of course, in vain. For psychology demands that each measurement shall deal with something specific and fairly homogeneous, and the record pertains only to the factor under control. Our gardener's measure of the quality of tomatoes may or may not represent a quality of his potatoes, peas, or roses. Each article must be measured by itself. So only when we have collected sufficient data to be assured that all the essential and fundamental traits of intelligence are represented, may we speak of an adequate measure of intelligence. The same principle applies to the measure of musical ability.

SIGNIFICANCE IN VOCATIONAL PSYCHOLOGY

Turning to the third question, as to the significance of a measure of a singer, we note that, if it is adequate, it places at the disposal of those who can profit by it a classified inventory of useful facts about this singer in such form that it may be of direct value. The advice based upon such an inventory should be weighed by the expert; the facts should be laid before the teacher, and the pupil should appreciate the self-knowledge thus obtained with reference to her possibilities as a singer as more extensive than could be learned by any other method. Her future career as a singer may be determined by this and similar knowledge. It may serve as an invoice serves the banker before he makes a large investment. If her case is promising the record is most stimulating and encouraging. If she is found to have some insuperable obstacle in the way of a musical career, the warning from the establishment of this fact may in a very true sense save life by preventing its wreckage upon the stage after long wasted effort. The record shows qualitatively and quantitatively whether she is by nature endowed with the mind and body of a natural singer; and it points out to her the fortes and weaknesses in her capacities and possibilities. It substitutes procedure with knowledge for the haphazard procedure so commonly followed in musical careers.

In giving and taking advice of this sort we

must, however, not forget the enormous resourcefulness of the human will, and the possession of latent powers. A one-legged man may become a rope dancer, a blind man a guide, a man with wretched voice an orator. Furthermore, art is possible only where there is willingness to overlook faults. A singer may be permanently lacking in some fundamental capacity and yet have such merits in other respects, or have such exceptional ability in covering faults, that she may be successful in spite of an overt handicap. But even then psychology has warned and explained.

This inventory also serves to explain experiences of the past which may not have been understood. If the singer has had defeat, it will show exactly why. If she has been misguided in musical training, it may show the nature of the error and its results. If the singer is conscious of lack in some capacity, the record shows the nature of this lack, and may even suggest a remedy, if such there is. Even among the best musicians it is rare to find one who does not have some kind of difficulty. Indeed, the difficulties of the singer are unquestionably great. If psychological measurement can lend assistance by laying bare the conditions of the difficulty and by determining its nature and extent; it will indeed be in this respect a handmaid of music.

MENTAL MEASUREMENT

It may also be of great value in discovering new singers who are not aware of their genuine ability.

Another effect of such measurements is not only to objectify the elements of musical appreciation and expression so as to deepen the insight of the expert, the teacher, and the pupil, but also to shape the science and art of music as the scientific conceptions gradually become known. The measurements will furnish an outline for the psychology of music.

From the very nature of his art, the musician as a rule takes the same kind of attitude toward his performance as an author of national reputation took to the Ouija board, which I had the pleasure of observing in action. In a certain sitting where the Ouija board was being shown I remarked upon the extraordinary quickness of the sitter's eye in reading the spelled words. "Eye," he said. "Do you think I use my eyes?" "Let us try it," I replied. "Close your eyes and proceed." Just as he began to write I slid the board an inch to the side, and, of course, the indicator, known as the "rider," did not get any words right. The performer was completely astonished. He had engaged in more than one hundred and fifty successful sittings, and yet he had not become aware of the fact that the use of his eyes was essential to his success. The message had come to him as a communication from without. The demand for so-called inspiration in music develops this attitude. The musician proceeds with a remarkable unconsciousness of the elements involved both in the appreciation and the performance of music. Any musician who is invited into the psychological laboratory where experiments in the psychology of music are performed will reveal this; it is an entirely natural fact and casts no reflection upon him. The psychology of music for musicians has not yet come into existence. Its coming depends upon the recognition that psychologists will give to the possibility of psychological measurements in music. The musician rightly waits for the psychologist to blaze the trail. The perspective of music, and the perspective of the musician, which is gained by the objectifying of factors involved, will be projected into our common account of music; and this will vitalize musical ideas and furnish the singer a more general insight into his capacities and possibilities.

Such features of the psychology of music will form a foundation for musical pedagogy. Some time ago the director of a great symphony orchestra brought his instrumental and vocal soloists into the psychological laboratory and there performed a large number of experiments on them. Everything proved practically new to these musicians, and yet they did not tire in pointing out what a great help each and every measurement would be in their training if it were available. Take one example— the measurement of the pitch of an instrumental or vocal tone as seen in the direct reading on an instrument, the tonoscope, in the laboratory. Orchestra leaders and soloists continually differ in regard to the pitch sung or played under given circumstances. The director called upon the players of the oboe, the French horn, and the first violin, in turn, and, the instant each played, the recording instrument showed, to a small fraction of a vibration, how much the tone played varied from the true tone, and disputes of long standing were settled in a moment. The conductor then proceeded in the same way with his vocal soloists. They all saw their faults and fortes pictured quantitatively on the instrument, and left the laboratory unanimous in the verdict that the introduction of such psychological measurements into the conservatory would be a great step in the advancement of musical instruction. To add just one more instance: a professional singer suspected that she sang flat. It took only twenty minutes in the laboratory to measure the characteristic amount of her flatting in representative parts of her register. Practicing for a short time with the measuring instrument would correct this tendency.

To develop measuring instruments and methods, and to standardize them, is the business of the psychological laboratory because, when the musician employs any of these measurements, he is employing psychological, and not musical, technique.

Measurements of this sort may be divided into four groups, according as they represent essentially measures of natural capacity, plasticity (i. e., capacity for learning), acquired skill, or knowledge. The art of music would profit by access to measurements in each and all of these aspects.

After all, psychology itself will be the chief gainer. One cannot observe under controlled conditions in a field so rich and unworked without gathering new facts, correcting errors, broadening views, and deepening insight into the nature of the mental processes involved in music. Applied psychology of music is to pure psychology of music as engineering is to physics; they must go hand in hand. Neither stands higher nor lower than the other in the rank of merit as a pursuit.

In conclusion, then, what is the lesson of our illustration? This forecast of a laboratory procedure in a particular case of applied psychology may be summed up in the following propositions:

Technical psychology may be so employed as to furnish qualitative and quantitative classified knowledge about a singer. The selection of measurements has here been made on the theory that measurements of the kind which we commonly accept in psychology may be so employed as to furnish a serviceable survey of the natural capacity, plasticity, skill, and knowledge possessed by a particular individual for a particular end.

This more or less exact knowledge may be so gathered as to serve immediate and directly practical purposes. We have insistent demands for applied psychology from the various arts, professions, and sciences. This illustration shows how one such demand may possibly be met. The effect of such an illustration should be to awaken confidence in our method, to enforce a wholesome respect for actual facts, and to ward off superficial and hasty promises of results.

Applied psychology, if such there is to be, must be experimental in method and spirit. It is the introduction of the principle of measurement that has given us a science of pure psychology; and there will be no science of applied psychology until the same principle is believed in and acted upon seriously by those who would make its applications. This does not imply a narrow insistence upon experiments everywhere, but rather a whole-hearted acceptance of the spirit of the experimental method.

There is need of consulting psychologists, trained in psychology and in the work to which it is to be applied, who shall devote themselves professionally to applied psychology. The field of the psychology of music is promising. We must not entertain the idea that applied psychology is to live merely upon the crumbs that fall from the table of pure psychology, nor that it can be reduced to a set of ready-made rules which may be handed down to the uninitiated. Applied psychology must recognize itself, its diversities, its stupendous difficulties, its essential limitations, and withal its promise and worth.

This attitude of modern psychology toward the human individual and the art of music will lead to a keener and more penetrating insight into the nature and the conditions of both the individual and his art; this will result in helpful guidance and a more vital appreciation and respect for the wondrous possibilities of the singer and the song.